Vessels of Honor

The Treasured Journey of

Bishop William and
Mother Hattie Hall

Published by:
Claire Aldin Publications
P.O. Box 453
Southfield, MI 48037
www.clairealdin.com

Library of Congress Control Number 2021918809

ISBN 978-1-954274-07-5 paperback
ISBN 978-1-954274-08-2 eBook

Printed in the United States.

Dedication

This book is dedicated to our four daughters, eight grandchildren, nine great-grandchildren and all of our spiritual children who are far too numerous to name or count. We love you and God bless you.

Acknowledgments

Our growth, both individually and as husband and wife, would not have been possible without the Almighty God providing guidance and directions to complete this book. To our Chief Apostle, the late Bishop William Lee Bonner, one of the greatest mentors and fathers in the gospel. To my beloved Pastor Henry IV and First Lady Pamela Davenport for their love and support. A special thanks to the following: Mother Barbara Pittman, who has been an inspiration throughout the completion of this book; Ms. Dorma McGruder, who sat down with us and wrote out our personal testimonies; Elder Michael Robinson for his recommendations and support; and finally to Dr. De'Andrea Matthews, founder and CEO of Claire Aldin Publications, LLC and her team.

Table of Contents

Letter from Chief Apostle Bishop William Lee Bonner

William and Hattie,

Solomon's Temple has been blessed to have you as an assistant pastor. When God spoke to me that you were to be my assistant, my heart was grateful. You took an immense load off of me in my absence while I traveled to New York, Washington D.C., Mississippi, South Carolina, aboard to Africa and other parts of the world.

William, you followed the vision the Lord gave me of appointing you as a full-time assistant pastor. I know it was difficult departing the pay wage and benefits you earned at your workplace. Not knowing or demanding for the church to meet those benefits was truly a man believing in God! When we were building the temple, I purchased the first stone panel that was made from "King Solomon's Mines" and you immediately bought the second panel. I sensed you wanted them to stand side by side.

Through the decades of labor at Solomon's Temple, you and Hattie have always been rooted in prayer, fasting, sacrifice, ministering to souls, servicing the people of God and dedicated to me. I watched your children grow up and I thank you for raising them in the fear of God. In the last days that we spent together, it was refreshing to know that my legacy rest assured in you and Bishop Henry Davenport; it will not die. Thank you for your commitment, service, labor, friendship, prayers, and tears. You have said it was your honor to serve me. No, my son, William and my daughter,

Hattie; it was my honor to serve as your mentor, father in the gospel, and most of all, your pastor.

My legacy lives on through you, Hattie, and Bishop and First Lady Pamela Davenport.

~Chief Apostle Bishop William Lee Bonner

Foreword

Can anyone find a greater assistant pastor than Bishop William G. Hall? We are currently living in perilous times. Every church wants "mega status," but they don't want to give mega sacrifice. We are living in times where the church has overlooked and erased boundaries. We want to be who God has *not* called us to be. Instead of feeding the flock, men of the cloth are covetous and seeking filthy lucre. We want what someone else has and will do whatever is necessary to get it. We fight over positions, power and prestige while the devil ransacks the church — stealing, killing, and destroying the sheep of God. The church is lukewarm, and even those in leadership will not accept correction — *If you don't do it my way, I will leave and find the latest and greatest!* Sadly, when the "cat's away, the mouse will play." You leave your church for a revival or vacation, and when you return, your church is unrecognizable. Korah rises up and develops a golden calf mentality. "Worship me! Pastor is not the only one God is speaking to in the church" — but not Bishop William G. Hall.

Can anyone find a greater assistant pastor than Bishop William G. Hall? Bishop William G. Hall is the epitome of a stellar assistant pastor. He is faithful and loyal to God and the people of God. Outside of normal services, you can find Bishop Hall at a hospital visitation, a funeral, passing out food, teaching a newcomer's or Bible class, or simply shooting hoops with neighboring youth. Bishop Hall operates behind the scenes. He has no desire to be lifted with pride; he is a humble servant. To God be all the glory!

Can anyone find a greater assistant pastor than Bishop William G. Hall? Most pastors worry about their assistant pastor rising up in error — changing the Word or the teachings of the church. Bishop Hall is solid like the Rock of Gibraltar. Sound in Word and doctrine, Bishop Hall will not be moved or easily swayed by the naysayers or those the enemy has purposely planted for the destruction of God's kingdom. I can leave town and return, and things will be flowing the same.

Can anyone find a greater assistant pastor than Bishop William G. Hall? Along with his faithfulness and being sound in Word and doctrine, Bishop Hall is a leader and follower. It takes great humility for a senior man to follow a younger man. Bishop Hall has given me nothing less than the utmost respect, for which I am truly grateful. Instead of him throwing his years of experience in my face, he often says, "You are the pastor, and I will follow." Not only that, but he said to me, "I will serve you just like I served Pastor Bonner." From that day to this day, I can truly say he has not reneged on his word.

In closing, I am extremely elated and honored to write this foreword for such a great man of God. He is my right-hand man, and I trust the God in him to the fullest. How many pastors can truly say these words without reservations? I'm so blessed! Last, this man of God is thoroughly qualified to write a book of this caliber because he's not just writing on what he knows, but also on what he has consistently demonstrated.

Can anyone find a greater assistant pastor than Bishop William G. Hall? You can search low or high, east and west, city to city, state to state, country to country, but you will *not* find another assistant pastor like Bishop William G. Hall!

~Bishop Henry Davenport, IV, Ph.D.
Pastor of Solomon's Temple

Letter to Mother Hattie Hall

"Who can find a virtuous woman? For her price is far above rubies."
Proverbs 31:10

The question was answered on February 12, 1982 when I met Mother Hattie Hall. The very first time I laid my eyes on her, she became special. I felt what I now know as the "anointing" of God all over her, as she in her sweet, calm tone told me to "Praise Him; He's giving you the Holy Ghost right now." I didn't quite understand what was going on, but it felt so good. Although I'm very cautious, for some strange reason, I believed her. Next thing I know, I was speaking in tongues as the Spirit gave the utterance. She was so excited; she listened to me for over an hour as I spoke in glossolalia, and for at least thirty minutes as I testified about the wonderful works of God. Oh, how patient she was! I immediately felt the love of God flowing from her.

This virtuous woman of God has been a tremendous blessing in my life. Her patience and love did not cease on the day I received the Holy Ghost. For the next four years before leaving for Nashville, she took me under her wings and nurtured me like a mother hen. She protected me from the wolves in sheep's clothing. She taught me the power of discernment. She taught me the do's and the don'ts—how to live holy, how to pray and fast, how to love the Word of God, how to be faithful, how to work with souls, and most importantly—how to love my Jesus! She not only taught me, but she lived it before me. Moreover, her spiritual repertoire can be humbly, yet equally compared with great Biblical women such as:

- Esther - her beauty (inside/out) and courage
- The Shunamite woman - her longing love for the lover of her soul
- Deborah - her wisdom
- Anna - her prayer life
- Priscilla - working with her husband and knows how to show people "the way of God more perfectly"
- Last but not least, Mary - highly favored and blessed among women.

In conclusion, Mother Hattie Hall, my spiritual mother, is the best! I am so honored to have her as the assistant pastor's wife of Solomon's Temple. I wouldn't want anyone else! Lady Hattie Hall, your works have spoken for you — loud and clear. My intimate thoughts of Mother Hattie Hall are finalized here:

"Many daughters have done virtuously, but thou excellest them all. Favour is deceitful, and beauty is vain: but a woman that feareth the Lord, she shall be praised. Give her of the fruit of her hands; and let her own works praise her in the gates." (Proverbs 31:29-31)

Passionately Submitted,
Lady Dr. Pamela J. Davenport, "Little Hattie"
(This name was given to me as a young woman by Mother Hall)

CHAPTER 1
Hattie Lee Jackson

I was born in Selma, Alabama to Hattie (Baldwin) Jackson and Peter Jackson. I was the eighth child of twenty-four children — their most unusual child. With twenty-four children — some stillborn, some dying after a few weeks, I was a born winner even though I did not know it. I was not her first-born daughter, but Mama named me after her. I believe she knew God ordained me to receive her gifts of prayer, and of serving and ministering to God's people, and I would continue the work after she went home to be with the Lord. God ordained me to be half of one of the greatest teams in the Pentecostal faith.

A country girl at heart, I've labored in the field, cut down trees, picked cotton and corn since I was five years old. As soon as we could hold the crops and were big enough to know grass from plants, my father put us to work in the field from sunup to sundown. Mama set the hens, the hens laid the eggs, and we gathered the eggs. She also taught us how to knock out hens by wringing its necks - the lifestyle of living on a farm. It was not easy, but it is good to know how to raise things and take care of yourself.

My parents used cedar and corn shucks to make chairs. Mama placed corn shucks in water, took them out, let them dry then wove them to make chair bottoms. Daddy knew how to bend and twist the cedar to make chairs and loveseats that white people bought for their families.

There was no electricity and no inside bathrooms in the country. We used lanterns for light to see; we cooked on a big, wood burning stove, fireplaces provided our heat and we had an outhouse for our bathroom. Mama taught me how to cook, but I always wanted to be better; so, I studied cooking in school. Mama was the best cook in the county. She cooked every holiday and white people would come from the city to have dinner with the Jacksons. That was during the time when black people were lynched, but my family was loved by these people, and nobody was allowed to bother or mistreat us.

Mama Taught Us How to Serve God

Even with all of our hard labor every day in the field, Mama made time to take us to church and teach us the way of the Lord. She believed in her children living, loving, working, standing and staying in the fear of God. Mama didn't play. She was firm and highly respected as the mother of our church. She taught us to never sit around idly. Our services began the moment we got there. If nobody was there to conduct service, we were responsible for handling every task. "Lee, I want you to pray, read the Scripture and explain it to the people. "Ruth, I want you to sing." "Lee" was my nickname with close family.

Each one of us had something to do and we did it well. When the preacher got there, service would already be in high gear. She taught us how to be missionaries. We could not eat right after church on Sundays. Once we left church, we had to visit the sick to see how they were doing. We tended to their needs, told them about our church service and what the preacher preached about. After all was done, then we could go home and have dinner.

I inherited Mama's most powerful gift: the gift of getting a prayer through! Anytime Mama was sick, I was the only one she asked to pray for her.

"Lee, pray for me," she always said, and I would pray. I never felt forced to pray or serve. I was born with the desire to worship God and serve His people.

Childhood Abuse and Suffering

Mama was always very soft and tender towards everyone. She wouldn't beat us; but Papa was a different story. Papa loved to beat Mama and all of the children using his fist or a long, tough, loud mule whip. He took his anger out on us whether we did anything to him or not. My older brothers and sisters said nothing because they were afraid of him. One of my brothers, who was a nice young man, stuttered in his speech, and Papa saw him as weak so he beat him a lot. He would beat us whenever he felt like it.

Some found excuses to lie on children so they could get in trouble and consequently get a whipping. Somebody lied on me and I knew I was going to get a beating. Although I put on double heavy stockings and a lot of clothes, Papa made me strip down to my underclothes.

I wanted to say something, but I didn't have the nerve. But one day, God rose up in me and I couldn't help myself. God gave me the strength and boldness to speak up. Surprisingly, it was not for myself; it was to defend the one person I loved more than anyone else in the whole world: my Mama. I heard all of this screaming and ran into the house. Papa had his hands on Mama and had grabbed a large item to hit her. I spoke with authority in my voice and said, "Papa, you are wrong! Don't do that no more!" He was so shocked at my boldness, but never laid hands on Mama again.

Wounded Heart

Mama had our future planned. When me and my sister, Ruth graduated from high school in the early 1950s, Mama showed us that she wanted us to move north to where some of our other siblings resided. She felt it was a great opportunity for us in finding a job that paid more than $25/week. She wanted us to have enough to save and buy a house so she could move with us.

Ruth had just finished pressing Mama's hair and was finishing dinner. Our cousin was on his way to take us on a mission to see about my sister's father-in-law who lived several miles away. I was about nineteen years old when Mama and I had what would be one of our last conversations. "Hattie, I want you to cook. I don't want Ruth in the kitchen. You know what? I'm feeling prettier and prettier every day. What time is it? 2:00 in the afternoon. My time to go. I'll be back."

She went to the outhouse. From the kitchen, I heard a loud funny noise outside and went to see what happened. I knocked on the outhouse door. Silence.

"Mama!" No answer.

Mama fell and was laying against the door. There was a lock inside the door and a hole next to the lock to allow someone outside to open the door in a case like this. I reached inside, unlocked the door and Mama fell out on the ground.

I got down on my knees and felt her wrist for a pulse like I learned in school. Nothing. I felt her neck. Nothing. I felt her heart. Nothing. When Mama and I did not come back to the house right away, Ruth came running out to see what happened. When she saw Mama on the ground and me on my knees next to her, she said, "I'm going to go back in the house and get a wet towel. It may make her feel better and come back." When she ran to get the wet towel, I got upset.

"Oh my God! Ain't nothing moving on my Mama!" I fell silent and did the only thing I could—listened for God's instructions. The Holy Spirit spoke to me and said, *"Pray."* All my life, the only thing I knew was prayer and when I pray, I give my all. I did what Mama taught me to do. But that day? I cried out to God harder than I ever did in my whole life.

"Lord, bring her back! You can do it! You can do it! Bring her back! Lord, let your blood cover her right now! Let her come back and say something to me! Lord, bring her back through and let her talk to me and give me something!" Suddenly, the

21

Holy Spirit spoke to me once again. *"Open your eyes. Feel her pulse, in the name of Jesus."* I opened my eyes, looked at Mama, felt her wrist for a pulse, and it was moving.

"Thank you, Jesus! Mama!" At that moment, she opened her eyes and was blinking at the sun. Mama woke up praying, and my heart overflowed.

"Lord, bless me."
"Mama, can you get up?"
"Yes, Lee." I took her hand and she got up. God brought her back.

Many people say God does not hear a sinner's prayer. I did not have the Holy Spirit; but I did have religion. God will raise people from the dead. We started walking back to the house. She stopped walking and turned to me with an expression I never saw before and would never forget.

"Lee, take care of my children." She saw my instinct of responsibility, and the duty of being the caregiver of our family would be passed to me through her. I believe she knew she would be dead before sunset. My cousin arrived and Ruth rode with them to take Mama to the hospital about eight miles away. Their car broke down, and a friend saw them on the road and took them the rest of the way. I stayed home to watch the younger children.

They were always slow to treat us because we were black. This time, the doctor never did come and see about my Mama. Papa wasn't home at the time, but somebody found him and told him what happened. He got to the hospital and went to the emergency room. He sat next to Mama's bed and held her hand. After a few minutes, Mama looked at Papa and spoke her last words.

"Brother Jack, turn my hand a loose! My Lord has come for me and I'm ready to go." And she died.

When they came back and told me my mama was dead, I was ready to die. I did not want to live if my Mama was gone. I felt like everything that mattered in my life was gone. That morning, Papa had just sharpened the double-bladed ax. I ran out of the house and fell across that ax. But God had His plan! I hoped I was dead. I stopped crying, got up and looked down expecting to see blood and my guts in my hands. However, the ax did not cut me anywhere. Wrapped in grief, I knew at that moment that I had to keep living. I didn't know what else to do except to cry.

The day of her funeral, I cried relentlessly. I didn't want to go, but I did because Mama taught me to be strong even through my tears. And I remembered my promise to Mama to take care of the other children. I girded up the loins of my mind and went ahead.

Hattie Lee Jackson, Detroit

I had to trust God for what I did not see in a new place. Once my sister Ruth and I arrived in Detroit, I got a job as a live-in housekeeper. My boss allowed me to go home on the weekends, go to church, see my family and return to work

23

Monday morning. My boss was mean in every sense of the word. She was verbally abusive and lacked patience. She was from the south and treated me like a slave. But I endured while working that job, just like I learned to endure in other areas of life.

When my aunt died, I told my boss that I was going south to the funeral. She did not like it because I *told* her instead of asking her for permission to go. She said, "You can't go unless I say you can go." I ignored her.

When I got there a family member was looking for me. "Somebody is on the phone and said for you to come back home." I took the phone.

"Hello?"
"You take the next bus and come back."
"We have not had the funeral yet. I will be back after the funeral."

I went to my aunt's funeral and returned to Detroit when I told her I would. When I got back, she laid me out. I said nothing; I just continued working. When I got to a telephone, I called Ruth and told her my plan.

"I have got to find another job. I don't like the way this lady talks to me." Ruth was looking for a job and had an interview at a rag factory. I went to that factory, met the supervisor and got hired on the spot!

The supervisor said, "I've got a job for you because your sister told me how you are suffering on that job. It is a piece working job, folding towels for men that are in the factory to wipe their sweat."

"Whatever you tell me to do, explain it to me and I can do it."
"*I feel you can do it!* Can you come in Monday?"
"Yes."

I started on that piece job, earning $75 a week depending on how many towels I folded. Nobody bothered me and I was no longer treated like a slave by a slave master!

CHAPTER 2
William G. Hall

Alabama

I was born in Birmingham, Alabama on December 27, 1930 at Hillman Hospital. Mama was only fifteen when she gave birth to me. My father was horribly abusive. One night while he was gone, Mama decided to leave; however, she could only take one of her children. She took me. Based on motherly instinct, it made more sense for her to take the arm baby and leave the oldest child. My sister, Louise was the arm baby and needed Mama more than I did. But God had a master plan.

My beloved mother, Sarah Jane Hall

The biblical meaning of the name *Sarah* is "lady, princess, princess of the multitude." My mother was a great lady and a princess to me. She was princess of the multitude through me. I would not have the biological or spiritual children I have were it not for Mama. She endured more than what I have seen any other woman take. Her major hope was a better life for her children. She asked little and gave all.

Broken and Wounded

I never knew my biological father. Nobody knows how much that hurt then and now — over eighty years later. A boy who grows up without a father lives with a hole in his mind, life and spirit that is the size and shape of his father. And it is never filled.

My mother taught me the best she could on how to be a man, but a woman can't do that because most of the time, she makes the mistake of being too soft, i.e., "Don't be getting hurt." What do you want him to do? Don't have him sitting in the house with his legs crossed like a little girl. Let him be a little boy. I prayed, asking God to give me understanding; but being taught by women instead of men made it difficult. But God saw me through.

Relationship with My Grandfather

I was raised primarily by my grandfather because Mama had to work. He was an alcoholic and left me at the house. He told me to sit in a room and don't even look out the window. I was only seven or eight years old. We had a big clock on the wall that you could hear — *tick, tock, tick, tock, tick, tock.* I was obedient because he was mean, and I was scared of him. I did not look out the window. Only God kept me. I didn't know God as a child, but I know now it was God who kept me from losing my mind and from being admitted to a mental hospital from listening to that clock ticking for hours every single day.

My grandfather was a farmer who grew corn, tomatoes, potatoes, red hot peppers, garlic and I had to work in the garden. There were tomato worms out there with big stickers on their backs like scorpions. The more they ate tomatoes, the bigger they got. I had to pick the worms off the tomatoes. I was afraid of the worms because they would stick you with their sticker and wanted to use a stick, but Granddaddy was mean and would not allow that. "Get them off with your hand," he would tell me.

He cooked and ate fresh fruit, fresh meat and fresh vegetables. His meals looked and smelled real good; not my meals. A lot of times, we had food left over for a couple of days or more that I had to eat. He would take that spoiled cornbread and those peas, and warm them up on the stove. He took red hot peppers and put them in the peas to kill the sour taste. He put them in a bowl, turn to me and say, "Eat it." Every day after I ate that sour food, he made me eat a piece of garlic.

"Why do I have to eat the garlic, Grandpa?"
"It's to kill the worms that will grow in you from the sour food you ate."

I was so scared of him because he was so mean to me. I did what I was told so I could hopefully avoid a beating. I was always big and strong for my age; but I was a coward, and I wouldn't fight. A boy used to hit me in my nose because my nose bled easily, and I would go home crying. One day, I came home with a bloody nose, and grandpa was waiting.

"You come in this house one more time with a bloody nose and I'm going to beat you!" That day, the boy didn't hit me in my nose. I knocked him around because I didn't want my grandfather doing anything to me.

William, Detroit

At some point, Mama remarried. My stepfather and I did not have a healthy relationship. While we were in Alabama, my stepfather went to Philadelphia to find work. He could not find work there, so he went to Detroit. When I was fourteen, Ford Motor Company hired my stepfather. He sent for us and we caught the train to Michigan in 1945. We lived near Grand Boulevard for less than a year, then we moved to Ferndale, west of Wyoming Avenue. They had built up a new community out there with two-story projects, an A & P Supermarket and a brand-new theater. I was part of the first class that graduated from the new school.

On the other side of Wyoming Avenue on Nine Mile Road was Lincoln High School, but I couldn't go there because we were out of the district. I had to be bussed to Sherrod Intermediate School on Cameron and Euclid, and I attended Northern High School. I was supposed to graduate in 1949. At that time, students made out their own program. Naturally, I took all of the easy classes I could find. Students had to have a certain amount of points to graduate. Although I exceeded the amount of points necessary for graduation, I didn't complete economics. I had to attend another semester, and then I graduated from Northern High School in 1950.

I had no self-esteem. I had no confidence or positive self-image. I was deeply affected by what my peers thought of me—even more by what they said about me. Right after high school, the fellows I grew up with got jobs in factories and I got a job at A & P Supermarket on Nine Mile Road and Livernois. They made fun of me working at A & P, and their words made my life look bad in my own eyes. In fact, I almost quit A & P and got a job in the factory! My stepfather was interested in me becoming a man and getting an education. I used to get upset with him because in those days, men didn't wear blue jeans and gym shoes; he made me wear a tie. My stepfather gave me wise advice in many areas and told me to stay with A & P.

My friends were making a large sum of money for a little while, but when they got laid off, I would be the one laughing. It turned out to be true because when they got laid off, they wanted to borrow money from me. My first job at A & P was a porter. I had to clean up, mop floors and wash windows. The Lord blessed me to be promoted to the grocery department putting up stock. From there, I was promoted to produce, then to the meat department. Every promotion meant more money.

Before I could get into the meat department, I had to learn how to cut meat. Meat cutting is skilled labor where other departments are semi-skilled. In those days, most meat cutters with A & P had to go to school to learn how to cut meat because they had to know bone structure. When I first went up there, they put me on fish and chicken. I watched the Hebrew boys and made a few mistakes, but I ultimately became a journeyman meat cutter without going to school. That is just like moving from an intern to being a doctor.

Before the meat cutter becomes a meat cutter, he is a butcher first. God had started teaching and I started learning His way. When I started with A & P, there were just a few blacks in management. Most blacks were porters because A & P practiced racial bias. But God put them into an unusual situation when it came to a small store at John R and Holbrook. They needed a meat manager and could not find

31

anybody white willing to go in the neighborhood. I was the only eligible black man at the time. I told my manager I did not want to go. He said otherwise.

"Go ahead and take it. It is a wonderful opportunity for you to move up the ladder."

I was angry because of how blacks in the community were being treated. With blatant racism, even in food quality and availability, we were forced to accept anything they provided. As long as the community did not complain about the rotten meat, they had a white manager down there. When we started complaining about the spoiled pig ears and pig tails, they want to send somebody Black there. That somebody was me. There were city and statewide weights and measures and the officials were constantly coming in the store trying to find things on me. Once I got a $500 ticket for inaccurate weights and measures because I did not weigh the package upright. The supervisor came in to fire me. The man under him, knew me and knew how loyal I was to the company.

"If you fire Bill Hall, you will have to fire me," the man told the supervisor. He didn't fire me. Even then, God was watching over me.

One day while we were in the meat department, there was a man in the store stealing meat. The thief had all of the employees backed up in the parking lot. Somebody said, "Go get Bill Hall to go after to him." They came and got me, and the man took off running down the alley. I ran after him, caught him and put a hammer lock on him. I was pretty strong. As they watched me grab and hold that man with my big hands and strong arms, someone said, "I'm so glad you got religion!"

I told the supervisor, "You are going to miss me because you will never get another Bill Hall. I did things from my heart. You will never get a man to stop working, run after a man, catch him and stop him from stealing your merchandise." They talked about that incident until I left A & P years later. My relationship with my stepfather felt set apart that I always felt distant from my cousins and other family members. We moved to a house on Princeton, located on the west side of Detroit. My stepfather taught me some good things. I was taught to obey adults. When asked by a neighbor to come across the street and help them, out of obedience, I went. My stepfather came back and found out I wasn't there with the rest of the children. When I got home, I got disciplined.

As a child, I saw and heard things that were hurtful, but it shaped the way I treat my wife and children—with unconditional love. God had a plan. At nineteen years old, I received a personal invitation: *Your Friends and Neighbors have selected you to serve in the United States Armed Forces.*

Korea

In 1948, Truman desegregated the Army. Despite desegregation, blacks were still in the back. I was drafted for twenty-four months from 1951 to 1953; but was on frontline combat duty in Korea which knocked three months off my service time. I trained in Fort Leonard Wood, Missouri, because their terrain is the same as the terrain in the far east, Korea and Japan.

When we got ready to rotate out, one hundred black and white men, all of the Blacks except one, were sent to Korea. We cried because we knew we were being sent to hell. One black soldier thought he escaped because he was sent to leadership school. After two weeks, he arrived in Korea. We laughed at him because we knew that he had to accept the fact he was no better than the rest of us. But most of the white soldiers were sent to Arizona to build airstrips for the planes and did not have to go to Korea. That was a prejudiced, racist practice.

I was a combat engineer, and we did not have serial numbers. Instead, we had a type of number that identifies you by what unit you are in. 1745 is a foot soldier, the one who goes out front. My number was 3745, which meant I was an engineer who cleared minefields, blew up railroad tracks and build bunkers. I lived, breathed, heard, saw, and constantly felt what no movie will ever accurately show. When you are with your Army brothers, one minute you see a man; then mortar rounds, which are nothing but small bombs, start coming in and the next minute you see arms, legs and heads flying in all directions. I did not know the Lord in a personal relationship, but I knew God was real. I never knew fear like that before or since, and I did what you do when you are living in that kind of fear. I prayed from the depths of my heart. "Lord, if you deliver me from this, I'll tell everybody how real and how good you are." And He did. But I didn't. He could have cut me off then. But He didn't. God had a plan—a master plan. Korea got worse.

I was building a bunker at 4:00 in the morning. It was so dark that you could not see your hand in front of your face. I had the sides up—one row of logs and one row of sandbags three feet deep. One of the guys lit a cigarette. The enemy spotted that tiny light and started throwing miniature bombs. Everybody ran into the bunker. I was last, and I did not have on my helmet. When I sat down, we took a direct hit in the bunker. I was sitting where the grenade came in on us and I was directly under the logs. The mortar round hit the logs and the logs split my skull open. The bunker caved in on us, and the last thing I heard was somebody yelling, *"Get him on the helicopter!"*

I had seven other wounds in the arm, leg, lip and nose lacerations. They didn't have proper facilities in Korea, so I was flown to a Japanese island, where they had a proper hospital to perform the operation to close my head. I told the nurses about the open wounds on my arm and leg, but they ignored me. They did not clean the wounds or change the bandages. I could smell my flesh rotting and they paid no attention to it because the G.I.'s were getting bombed one right behind the other and coming in fast. But there was blatant racism there, too. White soldiers who only got lacerations and other minor wounds were brought in. The nurses were pitter-pattering around with these guys and not paying any attention to me or any of the black soldiers who were more seriously wounded.

Finally, after several days of heat, screams of dying and wounded soldiers, the doctor came in and pulled back the bandages on my leg and arm. Gangrene had turned my flesh green, and my pain was excruciating! The doctor hollered at the nurse, then gave me two little white pills. I felt like I was floating off somewhere. They knocked me out really good. I thought they were going to take me into surgery and amputate my right arm and leg. Somehow, they took layers of skin and grafted it to cover, bind and heal this wound on my arm. On one of my legs, the gangrene had not set in as deep. They put that leg back together with wires instead of regular stitches. When it was time for them to be removed, there was no anesthesia, no preparation; they just snatched them out and the pain was unbelievable!

When they got ready to do surgery on my head, God had already started healing me. My skull was already healed and all they had to do was stitch my skin. I had a direct hit to my head, and my brain was exposed. I was supposed to be dead. That's why my buddies were so amazed and could not believe I survived.

"We saw your brains!" they exclaimed. I had to stay in that hospital for almost five months, but God blessed me to heal fast. Once I was healed, they sent me back up to the front line, and the white guys were sent home. God was in every aspect of my life. This healing was not scientific; it was all God. When I found out about my orders to go back to hell to get blown into pieces and sent home in a bag, I decided to end my life. Better I should end it than let the Army allow the enemy to take it!

Before I went in the Army, the strongest thing I've ever drank was H2O—just plain water. I tried to commit suicide by drinking two fifths of cognac and a case of beer. I drank enough to kill a man because I did not believe I would be able to come back. It was too strong, and it burned inside—but I did not die. I passed out with dry heaves; it felt like my insides were coming out. God blessed me to come back and rotate from Korea.

One morning, I was headed home with the police stopped me and threw me out of the car. I was a G.I.! They didn't care. If they suspected anything wrong about me, they were supposed to call the MPs. They were not supposed to handle a G.I. After they roughed me up, they finally told me why they stopped me.

"We thought you stole this vehicle."
"If I did, what are you roughing me up for? Why didn't you call MPs?"

They just let me go. They never apologized because they did not think they did anything wrong. For years, I had a hatred for police and said none of them were no good because of the way they treated me—a G.I.

I have told people time and time again about all eight of my wounds, especially the one in my head. When people would say, "There he is, getting up talking about Korea," that breaks my heart. I dealt with daily racism over there. There I am, getting shot full of holes *for us*. For them to make a statement like that says they don't care that my head got ripped open.

People just don't know what veterans have seen, suffered and endured for our country. When I was wearing my Korean veteran jacket, a white man stopped me.

"What are you doing? Wearing that for decoration?"

If it weren't for me, he would not have a job. When I hear statements like that, I don't care how much Holy Ghost you have. You'll want to get all the way in the flesh! But the grace of God kicked in and I let him walk away. I was in Korea two years and two days, and I sent my allotment home to my mother. She promised me to save my money so I would have it when I got home. I had planned to get my own place…but when I got home, there was no money. To this day, I have my suspicions of what happened; but I will never know for sure. Nobody ever told me, but one thing was true. There was no money. My money that I worked, sweated, risked my life for, almost got killed for, was looking forward to using to build a new life for myself, was gone.

CHAPTER 3
God Weaving Separate Lives Together

Hattie Hall

I always loved and served people; once I got to Detroit, I continued to follow my heart's desire to visit the sick and show love and respect to the needy. I did not have the gift of the Holy Ghost, but I did have a spiritual mind and I knew there was something else and was actively seeking my new place in God.

Ruth and I were attending Gregg Memorial Church on Log Cabin and Fenkell. One of our members was sick and I wanted to visit her to see if she needed anything.

"Ruth, let's go see Alfreda because she had her tonsils removed."

We stopped and bought a gallon of ice cream because Mama taught me to always take something when you go visit a sick person. While we were sitting in Alfreda's room, this man walked in—Alfreda's brother—William G. Hall. I was not a flirtatious woman. I was quiet and observant. But when I saw that man, something went all over me. I just could not help myself! "Oh, oh, oh I love that man!" But I didn't say it out loud. When we got ready to go home that evening, his kind, sweet mother expressed genuine concern for our safety, even though she just met us.

"It's getting dark and I don't like my children or any girls to walk out there by themselves. Let my son William drop you off."

I never looked at him. I didn't pay him any attention. When we were going to get in his car, I tried to tell Ruth to ride in the front seat.

"Go get in the car."
"I am not going to get in there first."

I got in first and sat in the front, and Ruth got in the back. He closed the door, we told him where we lived, said thank you and that was it. Until he looked over at me and asked me a question.

"Why are you sitting so close to the door?"
"This is where I am supposed to sit. That's giving you room over there." He said nothing else, but he kept looking at me.

"You better not kidnap us," I warned him.
"I ain't going to kidnap you."

We got home, said thank you and got out of his car. As soon as I got in the house, I told my other sister about William. I was so excited!

"Alfreda's got a little old brother over there and I love that man!"

"He has got to be something good because you never talk loud," she retorted.

The next time we went to visit, I still did not let him know I liked him. One time, I decided to call Freda to check on her. I hoped that young man was not thinking that I was trying to run after him. I was playing hard to get. I called her, he answered the phone and gave it to her. Then, he made his request known.

"When you get through talking, I want to talk to her."
"My brother said he wants to say something to you," Alfreda said.

While talking with William, we got into a debate about speaking French and Spanish after he asked me a question that I did not understand.

"I don't know."
"No Francais," he said.
"Those words you are saying, don't mean anything."
"They do."
"They don't. Look here, man. I got a book over here and I am looking it up and I don't see "No Francais"! I will call you back with what the word means."
"Let me come over and help you look it up," he said.
"Okay, you can come over for a little while."

Over 60 years later, we are still looking up *No Francais!*

90 Days: From Courtship to Marriage
William Hall

When she decided to cook for me, the first meal was fried chicken, greens, buttermilk cornbread, macaroni and cheese, candied yams, squash and banana pudding. Hattie is the reason I started eating vegetables. I still don't know what she does, but I have been eating squash and every other kind of vegetable since we met. When she cooks them, they are the best I have ever had, and hers are the only ones I will eat.

I never was a Casanova. I was just a plain young man who never knew his biological father. All teachings pertaining to a woman came from my mother. She taught me to always give the highest respect to the woman because she is somebody's sister, wife, mother, daughter. I treat women just like my mother taught me, and I give Hattie the highest respect. Eventually through conversation, I came out and asked Hattie two questions I needed answered before I could pursue her any further.

"Do you have a boyfriend?" I asked.
"No. I don't."

I had to ask for two reasons. I was always taught to not come between a boyfriend and girlfriend. If she was seeing somebody else, I was prepared to walk away. The other reason was because I had previously been disappointed by young ladies I took out when I thought I was the only one. Before I could turn my head, I would see them out with somebody else.

I believed in monogamous relationships, whether the couple was married or not. That is the way I was taught. I really was hoping she said no, and she did. I knew beyond any doubt that Hattie was the only woman for me. The feelings I had for her made me completely forget about my inferiority complex. It is truly unexplainable. It was the Lord's doing because I was very shy when it came to approaching girls because of my low self-esteem and bad inferiority complex. But something drew me to her. She made me feel good about me. That is how I knew she was the one.

Hattie Hall

He would not give up. The more I tried to push him away the more he came over. We went out walking at the ball field that he used to go to, got pop and watched them play ball. He asked what time I got off work and he came over and picked me up. At that time, I didn't know that just like I loved him on sight, he loved me on sight, and I didn't stand a chance. God was knitting our hearts, minds and lives together.

We went out riding in his car to the park. A lot of people were out there and we went to stand under a tree. While looking around, with all of the people there, William G. Hall asked me to marry him. I had only one thought. *Now Lord, how am I going to handle this?* So, I asked him a question.

"Do you know what you are saying? We just met. Let me tell you later."
"Can't you tell me something now?"
"Yes."

He gave me the ring.

William Saw No Reason to Wait

We met in April. I proposed in May. We got married June 6th. Hattie told her sister, Ruth. I told my sister, Alfreda. We went to Toledo and got married. There was no need to wait and nothing for anybody to say. After we got back from Toledo, her sister gave us a wedding reception. A woman at Hattie's job had an extra room, so she said we could stay with them until we could find a place. We stayed about two weeks, found an apartment, got furniture and I returned to work at A & P.

William Loving Hattie

I loved Hattie! I might not have been showing it the right way with all my heart, but from the moment I saw her, I loved her, and I never stopped! Hattie did not stand a chance of getting away from me. She was my wife! Not because of how she looked, although she was beautiful. Not because of what she said, although her conversation was filled with wisdom. But because of how she made me feel. All of my low self-esteem and self-doubt began to fall away when I met her. My love and devotion for her, and my belief in myself only deepened and grown richer over the decades. As her husband, I learned through experience that you can't just be husband and wife in a marriage. You have to stay boyfriend and girlfriend, which calls for romance. Not sex. Romance is the relationship adhesive.

What we did before we got married was romance. Romance pulled us together and must be done to keep us together. I still enjoy taking her out for lunch, buying her presents especially when it is *not* her birthday. These things usually stop when people get married. Men no longer help women up the steps or help them on with their coat. When you don't tell her, "Baby, I love you just as much," this gives an opening for the death of the marriage to begin. She is not receiving what she used to get, what she still needs, and believes she has to forget about romance, caring, tenderness and friendship with her husband.

Some men believe to keep her means keeping her full of babies, in the kitchen, wearing a Jemima head rag. But she still wants to go out and have nice things; she deserves to have nice things. One thing I wanted to do was buy Hattie a mink coat. Not a stole, not a jacket, not a ¾--but a full-length mink coat. Even if it meant spending my savings, I wanted to wrap my wife up in a full-length mink coat. I did not rest until I got one for her. When we go out to dinner, black and white people alike look at her hats and clothes and compliment her on what she is wearing. I love to keep her looking that way. Sisters have claimed Mother Hall's hats. Brothers have even claimed *her* and I'm still living.

Nobody — not even Hattie knows, how much I appreciate her. Only God knows. What if I had missed her? I don't want to think about what my life would have been like if I had missed this girl. If she doesn't know how much I love her, I will keep treating her like the queen she is. My queen!

Two Years - Untwined

At the time, we were inseparable; nothing could come between us. Our love for each other was knitted and woven tight. Everything was fine until Hattie got saved and God started putting His plan in motion. He set up a different path for me to come to Him, using Hattie. A method she nor I had ever seen before. It was something about her way of living that I did not want a part of, so I began to distance myself from her.

One day, the husband of a couple we enjoyed socializing with said, "Ain't nothing wrong with you having another woman on the side. I do, and my wife don't mind. You know we are close to each other like you and Hattie. You are entitled. You work. You treat your family nice and bring your money home. You deserve it."

And so it began; that was the beginning of me taking my wife through literal hell for two years! I *never* put my hands on her, but the verbal abuse and overall mean treatment was just as bad, if not worse, than physical abuse. I was running my mouth, but she was praying. I know that's what got to me. Her prayers were more penetrating to me than for her to fuss back. When I came home, instead of her worrying about where I was, she was getting up off her knees. She wore her knees out. I still loved her even though I knew I was hurting her.

She made me even angrier because she was being so kind to me. I loved her in spite of how I was treating her. I believe it was because of her love for me and God's love for us both that kept us together. The Lord would start talking to me in my language, like two guys talking. *"Man, what's wrong with you? Here you are out here wallowing in the mud and your wife is keeping herself clean for you."* This doesn't make any sense, and I really felt bad. But when you are wrapped up, tied up, and tangled up in sin, you can't help yourself. I would tell Hattie, "I'm going out with the fellas." She knew I was lying and would do what she did best. Pray! I had a praying wife, so I was in a battle I could not win.

You can't beat a praying woman. She took it; but she wasn't taking it lying down. She fought back. She never said it to me, but I saw the results. I can only imagine her saying, "I can't fight you, brother; but I can put somebody on you who can bring you to your knees." Every time I came in the house, all I heard was Jesus. Every time I left out, all I heard was Jesus. While Hattie was praying for me to come home, before I got saved, I would go down on Hastings Street to find a woman and couldn't find a woman nowhere. God hid every one of them. After I got saved, while I'm going to work and paying my bills, the women were everywhere looking for a man. I thought, "Where were you when I was looking?" Then I would laugh and go home to my wife, happy that the Lord delivered me!

Hattie Loving William

I loved William at first sight. We grew up in houses with arguing and fighting and we didn't like it. We decided even before we met each other, we would not have arguing in our home. We can resolve any problem peacefully. A couple years into our marriage, the Lord began to deal with me about my life, so I began to seek Him. He sanctified me and filled me with His Holy Spirit. I didn't realize then that the Lord was preparing us for our journey in ministry.

William was not pleased with me as a sanctified wife, but I continued to love and respect him as my husband. He lied to me and treated me bad in a lot of ways. He would smoke in the car and blow the smoke in my face. He would look at me and say, "Girl, you a good one!" I took so much but continued to call out his name before the Lord in prayer. I believed God and knew that at His appointed time, He was going to fill William with His Holy Spirit.

> *...if thou shalt hearken diligently unto the*
> *voice of the LORD thy God . . . all these blessings*
> *shall come on thee, and overtake thee...*
> *(Deuteronomy 28:1-2)*

Pays to Obey

I found an incredibly sweet walk with God. It proved to me that God will use any willing heart to accomplish His will. I remained obedient to what God said. After a while, William started going to church with me occasionally. His winning personality at church caused them to appoint him to be president of the usher board. God told me to stay at the Methodist church until He gave me the leading to leave because through my life, He would bring the Methodist into holiness.

One evening, me and another sister who received the Holy Spirit with me, were in the Methodist church tarrying with the pastor. We had been witnessing to him and praying with him prior. The pastor always taught against the baptism of the Holy Spirit. But this particular time he had a change of heart. A deacon unlocked the door where we were, came in and in a fit of anger began yelling at the pastor!

"What are you doing in here? All this here you done taught me, that ain't no such thing as speaking in tongues, and here you got all this mess going on!"

He complained so crudely toward us, we stopped—but just for that night. God used me to draw the people in that church to Him—most of them. Nevertheless, there was one woman talked so repulsively that the Lord gave her a change of heart. One day she called me.

"Sister Hall?"
"Yes."
"Would you do me a favor?"
"Yes."
"Do you have your car today?"
"No. But I could get it. I will ask my husband. What is it that you need?"
"I want what you have. I want you to take me to Clinton Street Greater Bethlehem Temple to be baptized in Jesus' name and tarry for the Holy Spirit."

I asked William if I could have the car. He never interfered with me working with souls and doing anything for the Kingdom of God.

He said okay. I picked her up and she got baptized and received the gift of the Holy Spirit that very day!

The Lord started directing me to leave the Methodist church and go to a sanctified church, but I didn't want to leave because of the offices I held in the church. I was a stewardess and they wore a pretty white dress with a round pillbox hat. The pastor always called the stewardess women to do prayer. Also, I was the secretary of the missionary department and appointed as superintendent of Sunday School. I was important in the Methodist church!

One Sunday morning, God told me to leave the Methodist church and showed me the sanctified church he wanted me go to. He even showed me what the preacher looked like and the song the choir will be singing. However, I went to my Methodist church for 6:00 a.m. prayer. I knew God told me to go to the sanctified church but I decided to go right after prayer. Meanwhile, the thought came to me that all the offices and the authority I had at the Methodist church made me say, I am going to stay.

So, I went back home and got dressed in my navy blue outfit and white hat and went to my church. On Monday morning, I was home and the Holy Spirit visited me.

"Your neighbor, Gail, who lives down the hall is sick. Go visit and pray for her."

She had a huge red lump under her arm. I took my blessed oil, anointed her and while I was praying, she said to me, "Sister Hall, I've got a lot of dirty laundry that need washing and I don't have anyone to help me." So while I was washing her clothes, God spoke to me. "*I told you to go to the sanctified church and you didn't do it. So, you will see.*"

All at once, my whole left side became paralyzed. I could barely talk, but I managed to say, "Gail, I've got to go home right now. I'll talk with you later." I could hardly say that to her, the pain was intolerable. I could barely walk; the pain was throbbing. I fell out on the floor and cried out to God.

"Jesus, when I prayed to you to heal my mother, you healed her. You healed others as well. Please Jesus, heal me." He still didn't remove the pain. All day Tuesday, the pain continued. Somewhere between late Tuesday and early Wednesday morning, I thought the Lord was going to take me out of here. I still was unable to eat since Monday. I cried out to the Lord one more time, acknowledging my disobedience.

"I'm sorry! I'm sorry! Jesus! If you heal my body, I will not go back to the Methodist church unless you direct me!" And when I made that promise to God from the depths of my heart, instantly, I received my deliverance. I was able to move my whole left side.

When God speaks to you, obey. Hearken to Him. Because He will make you do it some way or another. He will chasten you. I'm a living witness.

"Though he were a Son, yet learned he obedience
by the things which he suffered
Hebrews 5:8 KJV

CHAPTER 4
Spiritual Rebirths

William Hall

Sunday morning, September 18, 1960. I was out on the football field playing football. Usually, I play very well but this particular day, I was missing all the tackles and more. Nothing was going right. The guys I was playing with noticed and asked.

"Bill (name friends know me by) what's wrong with you?"
At that moment, a clear voice spoke to me only I could hear. *"I want you to go to church tonight and someone is coming in to get baptized and I want you to go up behind him and get baptized."*

"My mind is playing tricks on me," I thought. I went home and ate dinner then Hattie and I went over to my mother's house. She asked me if I was going to church that night.

"No. I will stay home and keep the baby so you can go."
When we left my mother's house, driving on the expressway, the Lord moved on me again.

"Hattie, do you think it's too late for me to go with you to church?"

"No! It's not too late."

As I was sitting in church holding my daughter, Kim, I heard the same voice spoke to me when I was on the football field earlier that day when that man walked past me.

"That's the man."

When Bishop (Elder then) Bonner had altar call, this man got up and walked past me to the altar to be baptized.

"Hold the baby Hattie, I've got to go to the altar."

The Holy Spirit spoke to Hattie. "Take the baby and say thank you, Jesus!"

After I stepped out into the aisle, it felt like someone had a rope around my waist pulling me. Bishop Bonner was still making altar call. I was picking up my feet and being pulled at the same time. As soon as I came in contact with his hand, it felt like electricity running down from his arm and up mine, like I had touched a live wire. But it was the anointing in the man of God. That day, I was baptized by the late Bishop Carmel Long. However the man, Mr. Lee, that the Lord showed me to follow to the altar, got dressed first, and stuck his foot in water and decided not to get baptized. Nevertheless, as I prepared to get baptized, the deacons asked him to reconsider and he refused. A month later, the man called the church. He was a hobo (drifter), slipped off a train and lost both of his legs. Had I not obeyed the voice of the Lord I would not want to imagine what would have happened to me.

Bishop Bonner was the first one to tarry with me. Also, the season altar workers were helping me on how to seek the Lord. I continued to tarry about a month. The enemy fought me, trying to hinder me. But on October 26, 1960, Hattie and I were sitting down eating breakfast and she begin to encourage me, telling me how to give myself over to the Lord, lean to the Lord and believe He will save you. Ask the Lord to take you mind off your thoughts.

That night we went to church, Hattie and Sister Pleasant tarried with me. As they continued to encourage, the more I started feeling something taking over my mouth and I begin to give over to the Lord and all of a sudden, I begin to speak in other tongues as God gave me the utterance. What a feeling I cannot express what joy that filled my soul! I jumped up and declared that I got it! I got the Holy Ghost!

After I received the Holy Spirit, I felt God wanted more of me. He kept speaking to me about preaching. I continued to fight against it because when I was in my teens, I attended church on Sundays and sometimes during the week. I would see preachers coming out of bars with women on each side of them. I knew that was not the kind of life that a preacher was supposed to live. One night in service the Holy Spirit came on me and knocked me to the floor. I fell with my arms stretched out and my feet crossed like Jesus was on the cross.

As God was speaking to me, I surrendered myself. He said, "Would you be willing to tell the whole world that I'm real?"

"Yes, Lord!"

"Would you be willing to tell Bubba (my stepfather) that I'm real?" Because of all those I had feared, the Lord wanted me to be willing to tell them how real He is.

"Yes, Lord!"

After I promised God, the Holy Spirit begin speaking through me in unknown tongues. I jumped up and started running all over the church. Bishop Bonner asked me a question.

"Hall, what was that when you were saying yes?" Wisdom was at work because God had already showed Bishop Bonner what was happening and yet he didn't tell me. Because the Lord dealt with me very heavily about being a preacher.

So I confessed to Bishop Bonner I was called to preach. His answer shocked me.

"I know it."
"Why didn't you tell me?"
"It wasn't for me to tell you. It was for you to know for yourself."

Sister Hattie Hall

Something was happening that I never experienced or heard about before. I prayed and asked the Lord, "What is it? Is something wrong with me?

One morning I got up, prepared William breakfast and lunch for work. After he left, I begin to pray and cry to the Lord once again. "Lord what's wrong with me?" He answered and gave me detailed instructions I was eager to obey.

"Remember the lady that visited your Methodist church? Talk with her, she'll let you know what's going on with you."

"Lord, I don't know her name?"

"Her name is Justine Pleasant, and she lives on LaSalle." LaSalle was the same street my oldest sister lived on.

"Lord, I don't know that lady."

"Get the telephone directory book, look her up and call her. Her name is Justine Pleasant. On LaSalle."

I called her and her husband answered the phone.

"Hello?"

"Do Justine Pleasant live there? She has long hair and is medium height and visited a church on Log Cabin Street?"

He gave her the phone. "Baby, what can I do for you?"
I mentioned to her what was happening with me and she asked me do I drive and I responded, "Yes, but my husband has the car and he's at work and I'm home with the baby.

She informed me how to take the bus from my place to her house. She treated me like I was family. After we talked, she said to me, "Baby, this day salvation is required of you."

"But I have already been converted."

"But there is a deeper depth and higher height in God wants you to have."

She mentioned to me about tarrying, seeking and receiving the baptism of the Holy Spirit, speaking in other tongues as the Spirit of God gives utterance.

"I'm ready! I'm willing! Whatever it takes!"

William and I moved to a two-family flat on Cortland and Linwood. St. Andrew's Methodist Church was across the street from us. They were having a mass tarrying service that night and I went while William stayed home with the baby. The Holy Spirit took control over me in the church basement, but I didn't know what to expect. It was packed with people and the people of Church of God in Christ (COGIC) were there tarrying with the souls.

Sister Pleasant personally worked with me as I continued to seek the Lord.

"Keep on praising Him, honey, God loves you. He cares about you. Hallelujah!"

All of a sudden, the anointing just lit me up inside and my tongue begin to change from hallelujah to unknown tongues. I knew I had the Holy Spirit, nobody told me but God himself!

"Let the redeemed of the LORD say so,
Whom he hath redeemed from the hand of the enemy;"
Psalm 107:2 KJV

I got up and shouted, "I got it! I got it! The members of the COGIC were shouting and praising God and Sister Pleasant was rejoicing. I felt so good I didn't know what to do with myself. I said I wasn't gonna tell nobody, but I couldn't keep it to myself. My soul felt so good, I stopped walking and started skipping home. In my mind, I could see nothing but beautiful flowers and green trees. I felt free and happier than I had ever been before. But then I got home.

As I walked up the steps, William heard me coming and opened the door. He looked at me and stared. Not having a mirror to see my reflection but I have since learned that when the Holy Spirit comes inside you, your countenance changes outside as well as your spirit inside.

"The Spirit of God has made me, and
The breath of the Almighty gives me life."
Job 33:4 ESV

CHAPTER 5
Challenges in the Ministry

Bishop William Hall

After accepting my calling to preach God's word, Bishop Bonner put me in charge over the rostrum. My life has never been the same. There were other ministers with more experience who were already working in the church. I felt unqualified for this honor and responsibility. But that was what God told Bishop Bonner to do. The other ministers and the church members did not hide the fact that they did not agree with Bishop Bonner implementing God's decision.

God gave Bishop Bonner confirmation that I was the one to work close to him. I felt the weight of the load he was carrying, even though he did not tell me and I did not know it all, but I was ready to do whatever I could to support. I had no ulterior motive.

> *...for man looketh on the outward appearance,*
> *but the LORD looketh on the heart.*
> *I Samuel 16:7 KJV*

On Sunday morning, July 2, 1961, Bishop Bonner was preaching, and the spirit of the Lord was moving mightily. One of the deacons approached the pulpit with a troublesome look on his face trying to get Bishop Bonner's attention to answer an important call in the church office. Bishop Bonner knew what it was; yet prayed he was wrong. Nevertheless, there was no reason to interrupt the service while the Spirit of God was in high gear. He left the pulpit praying that God would answer his prayer and heal one more time. It was not God's will this time. It was the one phone call he never wanted. Bishop Bonner returned to the rostrum with the expression of being cut by raw pain caused only by devastating, irrefutable, life-changing news.

His mentor, his father in the gospel----the man he loved, Bishop Robert Clarence Lawson, Sr., founder of the Churches Of Our Lord Jesus Christ of the Apostolic Faith and pastor of the mother church, Greater Refuge Temple (New York City) had died.

The church members of Greater Refuge Temple vowed to leave the organization if Bishop Bonner did not become their pastor. Bishop Bonner felt indebted to become the pastor of Greater Refuge Temple. He equalized his time between Detroit and New York because Detroit was the church he birthed, and he would not give it up to someone else.

This necessitated him flying between Detroit and New York frequently. He logged so many flying miles that by 1973, American Airlines presented him free, round trip, first-class airfare to anywhere the airlines flew, *for the rest of his life*.

The death of Bishop R. C. Lawson, Sr. immediately multiplied my responsibilities. In the absence of Bishop Bonner, I thought the church members were supposed to show up because I believed we were all there to serve God. When they did not show up, or worse—walked out when they saw Bishop Bonner was not there, I would leave off the rostrum crying. Bishop Bonner found out and I mentioned to him why I cried. He said to me what a father would say.

"Son, you can't make people come to church."

I did not quite understand that because I had the church in my heart. I didn't play; I took my responsibilities and commitment to God, Bishop Bonner and the church sincerely. Not to be seen, nor was I trying to outdo anyone. Just wanted to be pleasing to God and serve my pastor.

One particular Friday night youth service, Bishop Bonner was out of town. I was informed the youth pastor canceled the service. I felt led (by God) to go ahead with the service. We had tarrying service and there were three souls seeking the Lord who came real close in receiving the Holy Spirit. After I dismissed the service, the Lord showed me to have the three young people to come back to the altar and try one more time.

"Vanessa, come back to the altar."

Vanessa got up, and the Holy Spirit took over. She began to speak in tongues right where she stood. Then I called the next young person, and when she got to the altar on her knees, the Holy Spirit was all over her and she began to speak in unknown tongues as God gave the utterance. Once I called the third young lady, she tarried for while and eventually God spoke through her as well.

The youth pastor heard I had handled the youth service and he was not pleased. I would have assumed he would rejoice of knowing three souls were filled with the Holy Spirit. Instead, he confronted me but God covered me with the spirit of humility. I did not flinch, I did not back down, and I did not express any signs of fear.

I grew stronger spiritually; I knew I was in God's will because most importantly, three souls were birthed into the kingdom. The ego of that minister meant nothing to me.

After a while, I was ordained to be an elder. Ordinarily when ministers go for ordination to become an elder, they're ready to establish a church. Bishop Bonner asked me if I planned to start a church?

"Yes, I do plan to go out and start a church where I was raised in Ferndale on the other side of West Eight Mile Road."

"The Lord showed me He wants you to be my assistant pastor full time; however, you pray about it."

"Bishop Bonner, it's not that I don't aspire to pray. But if this is what the Lord showed you, then I have sufficient confidence to know it is His will and I desire to obey."

> For I know the thoughts that I think toward you,
> saith the LORD," thoughts of peace,
> and not of evil, to give you an expected end.
> Jeremiah 29:11 KJV

I put my trust in God and He met every need for me and my family, from then until this present day! Bishop Bonner would always tell the church members, "I thank God for William and Hattie."

Hattie and I stayed busy in the church; our main focus was winning souls for the kingdom of God. We didn't pay attention to the spirit of jealous people in the church, those who tried to dampen our ministry or fought against us. We continued to demonstrate love to them and not once did we disclose any of this to Bishop Bonner on how we were being treated in his absence in the church.

There's a passage that says, "Behind every great man is a great woman." That is especially true for the husband of the Proverbs 31 woman! That's me! Because Hattie serves and manages our home completely. She enables me to be a man of influence outside our home. She placed her relationship with God first; that's where she drew the strength for her noble character.

The negative experiences we received as children taught us to endure when accused of things although we were innocent. The mothers who loved us through the pain they were powerless to stop, demonstrated to us how to take everything to God, no matter what the condition. The deprivations and lack of money instilled in us the power of discipline which taught us what was truly important. The betrayals from those we held close taught us how to cling only to each other. The lies, plots for our destruction, threats on our lives from those we guided and supported through their own issues, taught us how to keep our own counsel. Everything did not teach us to pray but helped us learn how to get a prayer through and get the answer!

Bishop Bonner was the spiritual giant over all the Churches Of Our Lord Jesus Christ of the Apostolic Faith around the country and overseas. The Lord was blessing the /Detroit church in membership. He felt I needed additional support as the assistant pastor to lighten the load of responsibilities. It's good to know that Bishop Bonner appreciated my efforts and knew my intentions were honorable. I learned to endure hardness as a good soldier.

In the ministry you're faced with opposition. I reminded the ministers that the focus must be about bringing souls into the kingdom of God, not destroying each other or their church. It is crucial to be dedicated to the consecration of ministers' character. Their character has to be above their ministry because character is who and what they are. If you don't have good character and preach like the Apostle Paul, it won't take you anywhere.

> *...I am become as sounding brass, or a tinkling cymbal.*
> *I Corinthians 13:1 KJV*

Development must be more than the ability to preach. Their character development would be no different from mine just because they are a minister. Positive thinking and prayer are very effective and that is where it begins. Again, as a man think in his heart, so is he in his soul. Those thoughts are actually words in his mind to be expressed. The method of expression from preacher to teacher is the only difference between preaching and teaching. The adult self is representative of the inward person.

Typically, behavior is because of the attitude, which is the way you're thinking whether it is positive or negative. When the attitude is developed, it brings about behavior. And that behavior develops a character. So once the character is developed out of those processes, I can only say what I have created myself to be. You can't be anything else. If I had gone back to my thoughts which were negative, my attitude and behavior was going to be negative. God cannot correct that. The man has to correct his thinking.

For as he thinketh in his heart, so is he:
Proverbs 23:7

When I started visiting the sick/shut-in, I served alone. Then one of the brothers, Ellis Taylor joined me in visitations. One day, God said to me, "Take your wife from now on." He confirmed it because of what was needed to be done when visiting women.

Women with special needs, while praying for them, Hattie lays her hands on areas of the female and I lay my hands on her. People called us in the wee hours of the night and God protected our children until we returned from the visitation. Often God would touch the hearts of the saints and reveal our needs to them. They called us and offered their homes to assist in caring for our children while we served the needs of the people.

It took all of that to serve in that capacity. We continued giving our whole being, working together for the will of God. The visitations would range from 3 to 5 a day, not including the midnight calls. It was physically draining, but it was also spiritually, emotionally and mentally draining. When you pray, you give out virtue and strength. One of the brothers was at the point of death and his wife wanted us to come pray for him.

"William, are you going?"

"Hattie, I'm tired." She would start to cry.

"What's wrong?"

"I just got to go to see this person. They are lying at the point of death. Can't I just drop you off and go by myself?"

"Hattie, I can't go tonight."

Hattie got on her knees and told God on me! "Lord, he is not able to go. Bring the man on through the night. They said his eyes are set. Don't let him die. Let my husband get rest tonight."

That did not happen. I went into the room where she was praying.

"Hattie, get up. Get ready. We are going to visit and pray for the brother."

"William, he might be gone now, but we will see."

When you humble yourself, go on and do it, God will move. When we got to the hospital, there was no update or change in the brother. His eyes were still set. We walked in the room, and Hattie begin to pray on the side of the bed while I anointed him. The Holy Spirit told Hattie to open her eyes and look. The brother was looking around the room, his eyes were no longer gray. He lived five more years.

Mother Hattie Hall

My first assignment with Bishop Bonner was working with souls. So many people were telling Bishop Bonner about how well I encouraged them. It's the gift God gave me. I prayed and told the Lord to let Bishop Bonner see for himself. God even anointed my children when they were babies. I would lay them on the altar, point to myself, put my hands together in the prayer position, point to them, put my finger to my lips and begin working with the soul. I was saying to them: 1. Mama is going to pray. 2. You be quiet and they never cried when I was with a soul.

One day, a lady name Connie Wells came to tarry at the church. Bishop Bonner looked over at me and beckoned for me to come over to work with her. In my obedience, I walked over, and I was down on my knees working with her. I forgot Bishop Bonner was there and begin to minister and encourage her as God was directing me.

"Come on, baby. Keep your mind on Jesus. In the name Jesus. Let your blood prevail right now. Lord, I know you're able. Come on honey, you'll make it. Keep pressing."

That lady came right through with the Holy Spirit! Bishop Bonner looked at me and said what I will always remember. "From now on, anytime you see me working with a soul, you come work with me, Hattie. I like the way you encourage the soul."

Each of us has a gift that God has given us. His greatest desire is for you to have a relationship with Him. How? Through having a prayer life. Submission and consecration. There were times when we were confronted with those who thought that tarrying with souls is not necessary. Yes, it is possible to get the Holy Spirit without tarrying. All it takes is a made-up mind, a submissive heart and God will come into your life.

At one particular missionary meeting, it was said that we were working against Bishop Bonner, but he was unaware about this issue. I asked another church officer for permission to respond.

"Would you allow me to have something to say? Please?"

"Go on, Mother Hall. Please say what you want to say."

"You made a serious accusation. I am not trying to embarrass or disrespect you, but I want you to know Bishop Bonner has not stopped anyone from tarrying with souls. More so, he encourages souls to humble themselves so the Holy Spirit can come in their life." The error was admitted with an apology.

When Mother Bonner formed the International Ministers and Deacons' Wives Guild, I was voted in as vice president. I served nine years and that is longer than anyone had previously served. Dr. Celeste Johnson was a great inspiration to me in the guild while serving as vice president. Mother Bonner worked so hard to make the auxiliary effective. She would go and get dinners, set-up and I noticed most of the women would not offer their service to assist her. I could not understand how we would not assist the presider's wife. Being treated with disrespect made me fear a leadership position. But the Lord blessed me through the struggle. Also, I served locally as vice president of the Ministers and Deacons Wives Guild.

God honors submission and divine humility. He brought me to the point that I can give attention to anybody with animosity. I am not going to allow you to walk over me. The Lord has me in a spirit of forgiveness and I don't answer to man for what comes and goes. I didn't realize I had it until it presented itself when God presented me to those who mistreated me, and I felt nothing but love.

A member of the church asked me go to lunch with her, so I did. I talked to the Lord about her before I went because I did not like the way she acted with me or my husband; but felt that the Lord brought us together for a reason. We went to the Big Boy on Dequindre and Eight Mile Road. Her conversation surprised me, but I held back and listened. She began to tell me about my husband and his preferences with my appearance.

"Bishop Hall loves curls, and he loves the way I wear my curls. You should style your hair like mines and do some other things for him he likes that I know about."

I did not give her the answer she was expecting, but I gave her what was in my mind and heart.

"Well, when Bishop Hall and I met, he liked me like I was. He still loves the way I prepare myself and the way I look. Therefore, you don't have to tell me how to prepare myself to please my husband."

This woman requested private counseling sessions with my husband and repeatedly tried to entice him to get personally involved with her. Years later, God did something I will never forget. I didn't think hard of her, but she said nothing else to me about that. Nobody had to tell me to pray for her, but I did. I needed and asked Jesus to help me.

"Jesus, when I get around her, just help her and make me love her. I don't care what she does." When I got around that woman, I put my arms around her and always showed love. I greeted her. I whispered a prayer because she often was sick. Wherever she was hurting, God would put my hand right on the spot of pain. She always told me right after that she felt better, and she responded in disbelief.

"Mother Hall, you are an unusual woman. Why do you always show love to me? Why do you do that?"

"Because God is love and He wants us to love one another."

Years later, this woman was in the hospital, only a few hours from her death. She called for Bishop Hall and I to come and see her. When we arrived, she put all of her family out of the room and asked me to stand on one side of her bed and Bishop Hall on the other side — and she talked to me first!

"I'm getting ready to leave this world and I've got to get this off of me. Would you forgive me for how I tried to give myself to your husband and he wouldn't even bow?"

She looked at Bishop Hall. "You've got an unusual wife. I did everything I could and when I would try to come on to you, you never would heed to me. Anytime I came near me, she put her arms around me, hugged me, whispered a prayer for me and put her hands wherever I was hurting, and it would stop hurting. Bishop Hall, would you please forgive me?"

"I already have."

God did it so gracefully. The woman who gave me a very hard time, who tried to separate my husband and me, confessed and repented. Women were approaching my husband, but I never believed in arguing with him or the women. I would tell God about them. I did not worry because my husband and I are partners and work together in every area of our lives.

We are the help for our companion to stand and withstand. Stand means that there are some areas at a visitation that needs the assistance of the wife. Withstand means to endure hardness as a good soldier.

God taught us how to cope with situations, how to keep it to ourselves. When people bring their problems to us, God taught us how to counsel and pray with them, not publicize their situation.

I love so much working in the body of Christ, working in the field He has gifted and assigned me. I can sit very prayerfully, and the Spirit of God speaks to me and says, *"Look over there. See that person? They're very troubled today. Pray for them."*

I immediately bow my head, and start praying and soon, I would feel a deliverance. I get joy out of the Lord directing me like that for the souls of the people.

> *Can two walk together,*
> *Except they be agreed?*
> *Amos 3:3*

CHAPTER 6
Serving As Assistant Pastor and the Assistant's Wife

Bishop William and Mother Hattie Hall

When we were informed that Bishop Hall would become Bishop Bonner's assistant pastor, there wasn't any training literature, videos, or classes to show us the qualifications of the positions that we would fill. Being able to cope with authority, in this case the pastor, is not a task to be taken lightly! Yet, we did not anticipate the people and circumstances we would encounter as spiritual leaders. We had no one to teach us how to respond and react to situations that occurred in the church. In other words, there was no book written that outlined the duties and responsibilities of an assistant pastor and his wife. But God . . .

This book does not provide training, but it gives more than we had when we started. In this book, we explain how we grew and developed through what we faced, suffered, and still suffer today. We also talk about how we endured suffering, why we stayed, and how we became victorious through it all! Simply put, we want to tell you how God has brought us through. First, we learned directly from Him. We could not run from person to person. We had only God and each other to depend on to teach us how to effectively serve our pastor, and His people.

Bishop William Hall

When an individual assumes a position there must be a goal, and a vision. Let's look at a goal from a team perspective.

We'll use basketball as an example. The team has five players. There's a point guard, shooting guard, two forwards and a center. Note, each person that occupies a position has a specific role to play. In basketball, the shooting guard gets all the attention because he/she shoots and scores. Scoring is the goal of the game and is significant because the team with the most points win. So, the role of the scorer seems more important than the teammate who passes him/her the ball. Many times, fans and spectators want to give credit to the player who scores the most points, but not necessarily the team. However, if a teammate doesn't deliver good pass, the person shooting the ball may not score. The goal is the main thing, but it takes all five of them to achieve the goal, not one! For a church to operate at its full capacity everyone must stay in their roles if the goal is to be achieved.

As assistant pastor, I never tried to be the pastor. I stayed in my lane and operated in my role. I was told a few times that I wasn't assertive enough. Whenever the pastor was traveling, he scheduled programs that we were required to follow. I would never change the program. He is the leader; I am not the leader. I am an assistant to the leader, so I followed him and did not usurp his authority. At times, it was difficult for me to stay in the role of assistant pastor and not take the leadership role in the pastor's absence. Some would say "you are here all the time and Bishop Bonner is gone most of the time, so you are really the pastor. You are my pastor." Others would say "you are not the leader; I don't care how much you are taking the leader's place." I've had so many people try to tell me who I was and what I should be doing!

I never felt less of a man being a follower. A follower might stay there for a while, but then pride sets in because in trying to reach the goal while playing your role, you feel like your role is unimportant. I learned that to be a successful assistant pastor, you must pray, work as a team, keep your own counsel and *pray, pray, pray!*

When people reverenced me as the pastor I responded, no, I am not your pastor. If he never comes back, he is still your pastor. Some people were telling me that to cause me to fall, while others were sincere in what they believed. It was hard enough for a man to submit to another man because of pride, but it became extremely difficult when they saw me as their pastor. The scripture says, "Pride goes before destruction and a haughty spirit before a fall" (Proverbs 16:18, KJV). I never let people make me lose sight of my role, nor did I let them pull me away from my goal as assistant pastor. The grace of God was sufficient and enabled me to fulfill my role as assistant pastor, and because I stayed in my role, I have been successful.

Bishop Bonner was mistreated by so many who wanted his position. I heard him in prayer numerous times; he would be crying, laying on his face. That got to me. Spiritual warfare hurts. Bishop Bonner did not come to me and ask for prayer. He asked Hattie to pray for him, but as the assistants, we both prayed for our pastor. This was our role!

As assistants, we stood fast and held our position and supported our pastor and church. In the beginning, my help wasn't spiritual, it was in a natural sense, working with my hands. Yet, I did not know I had to go through spiritual warfare! Despite the raging warfare, I still wanted to help my pastor. I wanted to be part of Bishop Bonner's spiritual hands.

I have been offered the elite/upper-class lifestyle and exceeding amounts of money—if I was to leave Bishop Bonner. Some proposals came from outside of our organization, but ultimately from prominent administrators within the organization. Their aspiration of my wife and I to serve them was lacking in their own congregation. They wanted to do everything they could to undermine him, make him fall, move in, and destroy what God instructed him to dream, create and build. But my mother taught me obedience, faith in God and faithfulness to my church. The love, respect, admiration and loyalty that I had for God and Bishop Bonner made me always emphatically and willingly say no! Discretion and humility did not let me go to Bishop Bonner with these offers. He found out when those who approached me told him I would not leave. They did not know, even if they succeeded it would be a short-lived curse.

As the partridge sitteth on eggs, and hatcheth them not;
so he that getteth riches, and not by right,
shall leave them in the midst of his days,
and at his end shall be a fool.
Jeremiah 17:11 KJV

Solomon's Temple

I wanted to be part of Bishop Bonner's spiritual hands because he needed spiritual hands, feet, eyes, and ears. The

Apostle Paul put it like this – how can I say to the feet that I don't need you? The person who gives the orders needs the entire body (church members) to achieve the goal.

For as the body is one, and hath many members, ...
being many, are one body: so also is Christ.
But now are they many members, yet but one body.
Now ye are the body of Christ, and members in particular.
I Corinthians 12:12, 20, 27 KJV

When Bishop Bonner was laying hands during a prayer line, someone must organize the people, sing, hold the bottle of oil, and pray for him. Everyone must do something; he can't do it all by himself. Like the body, the only way to be effective is to use every member of the body. All members in our natural body work together in unison. None of our members can say, "I don't need you." Your mouth doesn't say to your eye, "I don't need you." You can't see with your mouth or talk through your eyes. All members are needed!

When Bishop Bonner dedicated Solomon's Temple, he threw a bottle of oil against the church building during the service. However, he could not have built and finished the temple without everyone serving in their role and supporting the goal. The goal is the most important thing. Our goal was to win souls to Christ. If we worked together as a team, we were in God's will and the goal would be accomplished.

Elevation to Bishop

Bishop Bonner asked me to apply to be elevated to bishop even though I did not want or need the title. So being obedient to my pastor, I applied several times and was denied each time because I had not established churches or completed classes at the W. L. Bonner Bible College in Columbia, South Carolina. I applied again and was denied. I don't even remember why I was denied the third time. What was interesting is that the same administration who denied my elevation to the office of bishop were the same ones who over the years said:

"Hall, don't you think it is about time for you to leave Bonner and start your own church?"

"Hall, you are such an excellent teacher. You need to be in my church as my assistant pastor. Bonner is not paying you right, but I will."

"Hall, you really know how to run a church. You need to be my assistant pastor."

Bishop Bonner asked me to try one more time and I did. The fourth time, I was granted elevation to bishop. My son-in-law, Elder Vincent Geter, has an interesting perspective.

"This elevation to bishop for my father-in-law is long overdue. He has worked and served God all these years and never asked for anything. He teaches from the Word in such a way that you are never the same. His work, character, and reputation are blameless. He is always well prayed, well-read, well-studied, well-prepared. He says what he means, stands on God's Word and lives what he believes. The Church of Our Lord Jesus Christ is richer because of his sacrifice, prayer and continuous study and presentation of God's

Word. He exemplifies everything that a husband, father, father-in-law and bishop should be. His prayer life, wise counsel, unlimited conversations have made all the difference in the growth and strength of my pastoring and every aspect of my ministry, our marriage and family. This is a blessing from God. He did not seek it. But he surely has earned it."

God's Strength Made Perfect in My Weakness

God's grace and strength are needed do the work of a minister. God's strength really enabled us to do the extraordinary. *Spiritually.* At the same time, we needed His word, not only to quote it, but experience it, and live it! God's Spirit, His grace and His word are needed because spiritual warfare hurts and sometimes makes us stubborn. But without it, we would not grow and develop or become what He wants us to become, spiritual giants! If God places you in a position for a length of the time, it is evident that He placed you and not yourself! Just like He placed the stars in heaven by the word of God, he placed me where I am. If I say, *I did this or I did that*, I would be taking the glory for myself. But I must give God the glory. It's all Him. It's Him who has kept me and gave me His grace to endure the suffering down through the years. I was always taught to be obedient and faithful. When a person is faithful, they might get knocked down, but God is not going to let them get knocked out. I'm not going to lay down there. I'm going to get up and fight some more.

When I was in high school, the coach deliberately put me in front of a man twice my size. I would run up against him and bounce off him like a rubber ball, but I didn't let that discourage me. Even though the coach kept saying, "Come on

Hall, you can do it," that was not what made the difference in me not quitting. What really urged me to get up and try again was him standing there and laughing at me. You don't laugh at me, Buddy. So, each time I bounced like a rubber ball, I ran against him harder. Eventually, in my continuous trying and being faithful, I moved him. While you are standing, don't give up, you wait upon the Lord! I want you to know God kept me and protected through my faithfulness because people were giving me a rough time all over the country.

But they that wait upon the LORD shall renew their strength; they shall mount up with wings as eagles; they shall run, and not be weary; and they shall walk, and not faint.
Isaiah 40:31 KJV

John speaks about every branch abiding in Jesus, will bring forth fruit, more fruit and much fruit. We apply that to the lay member, but it is to the preacher. Lay members do not bear fruit. Preachers bear fruit abiding in the vine; Jesus is the vine. The reason it is for the pastor is because the pastor makes it bring forth fruit, much fruit, and more fruit. The only way I can be strong is to completely surrender to God and open my heart, soul, mind, spirit, life, words, and thoughts to Him. When I do that, He replaces my weakness, suffering, pain, tears, and mistreatment with His strength. But that *only* happens through my suffering! That is the only time His grace can be fully manifested in me. Once I do that, I feel His strength and I am stronger than any man because I am now operating in the strength of God.

I am the true vine, and my Father is the husbandman.
I am the vine, ye are the branches:
John 15:1, 5 KJV

Mother Hattie Hall

I had to prepare to be the assistant pastor's wife. "This church is going to bless the city." That is what Bishop Bonner continuously told the entire congregation. God told us to continue working and allow Him to use us. We were anchored in the Lord and obedient to our pastor. Many people say God does not talk to people in an audible voice. That is not true! God talks to whomever He chooses. He would give me instructions every morning and I was fully obedient.

"I want you to go to the hospital this morning and I want you to go now."

He would give me the person's name and the name of the hospital, and I went. When God says go, drop whatever you are doing because God knows what you are doing, and He expects you to do what He said. This was Jesus' command when He called His disciples to do His work. Even when they did not know who He was, He spoke with such power and authority, and they dropped their nets, followed Him and did whatever He told them to do. This is what it takes. A strong spirit of total obedience. I listen to God as I walk and pray.

He that hath an ear, let him hear
what the Spirit saith unto the churches.
Revelation 2:17 KJV

Who is the church? We are the church. Because of my obedience, God even gave me the desires of my heart.

"If you hearken unto my word and obey my commandments, I'm going to bless your household."

"Lord, you mean to tell me that I've got two children now and if there are some more to come, you mean you are going to bless all of them?"

"I will bless your household."

God began to speak to my heart and show me how to go forward in this walk because I didn't know what to do. The only thing I knew to do was go to God and ask Him to guide me and direct me. I went to Him immediately, but the learning and direction did not come overnight. Over fifty years later, I am still learning. I had to cry a lot because many did not want to accept us, but some did. However, being an assistant pastor's wife is not easy.

It was hard in one way because of the women. When I called for a closed session with the pastor's wives, some spread venom to others saying things like, "She doesn't know what she is doing." They didn't know that I had gone to Jesus and asked Him for strength and direction. I had to learn how to deal with obstacles, attitudes, hatred from people in my face and behind my back. I kept it all to myself and looked to God for direction. I had to ask Him to show me how to speak to them in the right tone of speech. I had to go through all of this to learn how to work with the people of God.

When people spoke hard and mean to me, the only response I gave them was, "We will pray on it." I had to endure a lot of suffering because of the words that came out of the mouths of people. I was repeatedly lied on. They went to Bishop Bonner concerning me and what I did. I did not go to him to try to defend myself or explain my position because I had not done anything wrong. They were lying! Instead, I told God to reveal it to Bishop Bonner and help him see the truth. God did just what I asked and every time, he found out the report he got was wrong.

I fasted. Fasting doesn't give you what you want. Fasting conditions you for the situations that you're going through. Fasting humbles the flesh so that God can take control, give peace and direction. Every single morning, my husband and I prayed. Not exactly at the same time, but very early every morning, between 3:00 a.m. and 4:00 a.m. We both will be on the floor, on each side of the bed, calling out to God. When I do things that please my husband, I keep doing them and improve on what I'm doing. I am supposed to be a help and support to him, not fight against him. I wanted to help him meet his obligations.

We are troubled on every side, yet not distressed;
we are perplexed, but not in despair; Persecuted, but not forsaken;
cast down, but not destroyed; Always bearing about in the body

the dying of the Lord Jesus,
that the life also of Jesus might be made manifest in our body.
2 Corinthians 4:8-10 KJV

When you submit and humble yourself before God, he reveals the essence of prayer and the importance of spending time with Him. I can't miss a day without prayer…it's a must! I learned I must not just express my thoughts and needs to God, but listen for Him to speak. When you seek God, you will hear His voice.

Remember no prayer, no power. Little prayer, little power. Much prayer, much power.

CHAPTER 7
Bishop William Hall – Teaching

The Holy Spirit gifted me with that deep, inner conviction of teaching in my heart. Preaching is proclaiming the Word of God. I don't believe all men are called to preach. All of these are gifts that are placed in the church for the perfecting of the saints. So, my becoming a teacher is the doing of the Holy Spirit. I had nothing to do with it. It's not like a profession that one chooses when you are in school. It is a calling directly from God. I taught God's Word instead of preaching. That is a calling, a love and an anointing because not everybody can teach. But one thing is for sure. I was determined to give all I had to God so He could make me the best that I could be at whatever I did.

Meat Cutter – Not Butcher

A butcher is like an intern. An intern is in training to be a doctor. But the word butcher – if you look at it actually means butcher. You can call a man off the street and bring him in the meat department, give him an apron and knife and he is paid to just cut up meat, any kind of way.

Meat cutting means you learn the animal's body, break his body down and learn his bone structure. When I take a beef line, which is the back part, I have to know the bone structure so that when I cut the meat, I won't cut it so the bone doesn't come out bigger than it should. If that happens, it's because it was cut at the wrong angle. You must know the bone structure just like the doctor who passes his internship and residency.

When a doctor is licensed, he really knows what he is doing. He is not guessing. He operates on a person and knows what he is doing because of his training. As a meat cutter, I am an "M.D." who knows how to cut a piece of meat like beef loin, and it comes out as a beautiful steak.

If your gifts are not used for the perfecting of the saints and you are not giving your best, they mean nothing. When the gospel, which is the power of God unto salvation, is preached, it is talked about for a few minutes in a one-way presentation after music, testimony and offering. It excites us and we listen for a while. Teaching is more effective because participants must research, do homework, think about and discuss content. When we study the gospel or any subject, we remember. I can do both, but teaching is the gift God birthed in me for the perfecting of His saints. I prefer it because it is lasting. According to the Bible, both are important because the gospel cannot only be proclaimed. It also needs to be explained.

How Bishop Hall Prepares to Teach

The first thing I do is spend time praying, asking for the Lord to lead me, guide me, direct me and give me knowledge to teach what He wants the people to listen to and learn. I ask Him to help the people learn. I can teach you, but no teacher can learn for you. You have to learn for yourself.

There are four necessary steps to learning:
1. Knowledge, wisdom and understanding of His Word
2. Comprehension
3. Analysis
4. Application

Once those four steps are taken in that order, your learning will become much easier because it is your method to learn to use. When you use these four steps, you discover that you are learning because the application gives you deeper knowledge. You can have knowledge from a book, but experience always supersedes what you memorize. The Holy Spirit comes to lead, guide and direct you into truth. Once I apply it to my own life and thoughts, I won't forget. But knowledge is not enough. That's why God's Word tells us:

Even so the things of God knoweth no man.
...that we might know the things that are freely
given to us of God.
I Corinthians 2:11-12 KJV

That's why the natural man cannot receive things of the Spirit of God. Because through his intellectual mind of knowing God without His spirit, he can only know natural things. Man is body, soul and spirit. He is actually a living soul that has a body and spirit. Human spirit, not Holy Spirit.

The Attitude of The Teacher

Being a teacher means having the ability to teach people and as the teacher, it must be done in the right spirit. This is the way I reach people through reading His Word and trying to get it embedded within them. I study to anchor myself in doing God's will because so much responsibility is required in teaching. I teach ministers who have knowledge and ability to teach, but they're in the wrong spirit which opens the door for arrogance. His spirit will look down on his students, they will feel it and God will not bless him, his teaching or the students.

You never get to the place that you know everything. He teaches to challenge His students so they research, write, answer questions, learn and retain the information. But that still has to be done with humility because the teacher is not there to stump or belittle the people.

> *And God hath set some in the church, first apostles,*
> *secondarily prophets, thirdly teachers, after that*
> *miracles, then gifts of healings, help, governments,*
> *diversities of tongues.*
> *I Corinthians 12:28 KJV*

The blessing of teaching is that it makes students ask and allows the teacher to answer such questions as: Who is the passage written for? What is it saying? What is the time of the writing? Where is it taking place? What was the language of that day in that place? Attitudes can't handle special gifts. Lucifer nor Nebuchadnezzar could handle them. God put them in those positions. They were to draw people and share God's goodness and power. They got full of themselves and God brought them down into destruction!

CHAPTER 8
Prayer Warrior

Bishop Bonner was in prayer before teaching a class at the church on the corner of Halleck and Dequindre. God spoke to him. At the same time, when I got ready to leave home that morning, the Holy Spirit spoke to me----with a force!

"You are my praying mother! You are my praying mother."

I could only think and question God in my mind. Where am I getting this from? Is my mind playing tricks on me? I am continually praying and asking God to overshadow my house with my two children, while we are gone. Prayer is part of all that I know. Why am I hearing this in my heart and mind?

Bishop Bonner taught Bible classes every day when the church was on Halleck and Dequindre. He was on his face, in prayer, waiting for the church members so he could teach. This day, after he finished teaching, he told us what God said to him.

"I want to tell you all something that the Lord showed me this morning while I was praying. Sister Hall is a praying mother. God showed it to me."

I said to myself, *now how did he get that from the same voice talking to me at home? How did he get it?* Later, I went to him and asked him.
"How did you get that Bishop? Because I didn't tell you and the Lord told me the same words at home this morning." He

said the same thing to me that he said to the class. "The Lord told me."

He placed me immediately in the missionary department without me going through the junior missionary department. Mother Pandora Williams was president over the junior missionary department, and he told her to work with me even though I was to serve with the senior missionaries. I took my new responsibilities to heart and gave my best to teaching new souls how to walk with God, how to do His will and how to stand firm in the Lord. Rest assured, the teaching they received from me stayed with them.

My husband says I am in a real sense like Bishop Bonner. He did not get degrees from psychology, sociology or theology; but he received his degrees from "kneeology." I think he is right. When the missionaries I trained became members of the senior missionaries, Mother Pandora Williams admitted, "I don't have to worry about them; Sister Hall taught them. When Sister Hall teaches them, they are taught better than anybody with degrees.

Mother Hattie Hall's God-Given Gift of Working with Souls

And he said unto them,
follow me, and I will make you fishers of men.
Matthew 4:19 KJV

I received the same message. He made me a fisher of men. I always had a love for people and that love exploded into the desire to treat people nice and help them, no matter who they are. I saw a problem going on with the children in our apartment building. I always had a desire to work with children, especially mis-behaved children in the neighborhood because they need it most.

The Lord told me, *"You know what to do. Get your Bible storybooks. Read to them. Talk to them."* Those children loved those stories so much, they would ask me to come every day.

"Mrs. Hall, are you going to meet with us tomorrow?"

"Yes. What time do you want me to meet with you tomorrow?"

They loved me reading Bible stories to them. I allowed them to ask questions and took my time to explain the whole story to them where they could understand it all at their level. It took root and they began to change. That's why mothers and fathers need to train their children, bring them up in the fear of God and tell them how good God is to them. Most of all, tell them how much God loves them. I used to bring them to Sunday School. Even when they stopped coming with me, they went to church when they grew up.

God gifted me with a love for laboring with souls in every capacity before and after they received the gift of the Holy Spirit. I don't know when I first discovered I had that particular gift; all I know is that God continues to stir the gift in me.

When the senior mother of the church was tarrying with a soul and their mind was not where it needed to be, I would start praying.

"Lord, bring their mind to where it needs to be."

Suddenly, which I am sure now God was directing me, when I opened my eyes and looked at her (mother), she beckoned for me to come work with her. It was confirmation from God, as soon as I got to her, the Holy Spirit started moving. The soul completely gave over itself to Him and they spoke in tongues.

When Bishop Bonner called my husband from his job, I got to be passionate – completely devoted to nothing but souls. I asked the Lord, *show me how, teach me, take control of my tongue Lord; Don't let me talk too much. Whatever it takes, let me serve you and your people wholeheartedly.*

This kind of love, gift and power emanates from God alone. Without Him, we can do nothing. The love that I have for working with souls, God gave it to me. So many souls were being filled with the Holy Spirit and speaking in tongues when I tarried with them.

Midnight Prayer

Bishop Bonner was going to Africa to complete the work his father in the gospel had started. He asked me to be responsible for conducting prayer service for a specific time.

"Hattie, I want you and the missionaries to pray for me because I have to cut down trees and build buildings, and the heat from the sun drains all my strength from me."

"What do you want me to do with the missionaries?"

"Have a midnight prayer. While it is 6:00 a.m. in Africa, it will be midnight here. I will be starting my day, I need you all to be praying for me at midnight. While you're praying for a few hours, that will get me through toughest part of the day."

Bishop Hall was right by my side as always while we did what God said.

"Lord, I ain't going to have nobody to meet with and I don't want to go by myself."

But I was obedient. When Bishop Bonner left for Africa, I started telling people to come to the midnight prayer for the pastor. The first time, it was sixty-five people and we started midnight prayer.

At first it was from midnight to 3:00 a.m. It quickly turned into all-night prayer! I wanted it to continue after Bishop Bonner returned from Africa because God showed me, through this prayer, many homes were going to be brought together. *Many souls are out there, and it will be a blessing for the people and I can help them! I want to do it!* Prayer can fix every situation. Prayer can reach to the highest mountain. If prayer can reach my husband and Bishop Bonner in Africa, prayer is that powerful!

Prayer – Suicide Prevention

God moved on me and Sister Linda James so we agreed to meet at the church at 6:00 a.m. several mornings. Even though I knew it was God, I still respected my husband for his permission. He agreed that it was okay with him as long as there a guard there to watch the church to make sure it was secure and safe. God would touch the hearts and minds of people planning to commit suicide and show them their way out.

A young man who was a member of Greater Grace Temple, left his job because he and his wife split up and he made his decision. "I'm going to Belle Isle and I'm going to end my life right now. I'm tired and I ain't going back to that house." God intervened just before he got ready to jump.

"There is prayer meeting going on at Solomon's Temple. Before you jump in the river, go to the church."

The man came to the church and asked the guard how to get to the prayer room because he was ready to end his life. The guard called me and said there was a young man there who needed prayer.

"Let him come in!"

He came in got down on his knees and I started talking to him. I asked him what would cost most, his life or what he was going to do? I started encouraging him and tarried with him, reminding him of how much God loves him.

"Come on brother, you can make it! You can make it!"

Before we knew anything, that man started speaking in tongues! Oh, the joy of the Lord that flooded his soul! It was a beautiful sight as he began to speak to me.

"Thank you, Mother. Thank you, Sister. I'm going home to my wife."

A bishop's sister-in-law took all she could stand, was at the end of her rope and ready to take her life. But God!

"Get you a cab and go by the church where they are having prayer."

That girl came to the church by faith with not enough money to pay the cab fare and asked me if I would pay the cab and I did. We tarried with her and she received the Holy Spirit in no time.

When you are pushed to commit suicide, you believe there is no way out. You are all alone and you feel God has turned His back on you. The Lord uses prayer and that prayer room was the cure to all who came with an issue. Resolved!

We had a dry season when no one was coming to the upper room to seek the Lord. I was not pleased with that and begin to pray.

"Lord, send some souls!"

I looked up, there were people with all kinds of issues coming (drug addicts, alcoholics, educated) in the upper room. I just love the Lord! I love and desire souls for Christ. It is a thirsty desire; just like you need water to survive; that's how I am thirsty for people to receive God's Holy Spirit.

A friend of Bishop Bonner who was a well-dressed man was attending the church. He was not a man you could easily approach. Some people were afraid of him. I spoke to him, "Brother Nathaniel, the Lord has spoken to my heart and he told me to tell you it's time for you to give up and turn to him."

"When do you want me to come and tarry?"

God gave me a humble spirit to easily influence a person. So when we press ourselves to the seeker, we give them the process of direction as God gives it to us then they will comprehend it better.

God used my suffering and endurance as the primary instrument to bring my husband into salvation. The suffering of those hurting women led me to counsel them in similar areas, yet each one was different. I told the women how to keep their house clean and always keep food ready. They should keep the children clean and teach them to be well behaved. This was not only important to maintain peace and a pleasant home environment, but children needed to know right from wrong. Mothers are the primary teachers and builders of character, integrity and salvation. Whether their husband was called to serve as a deacon or minister, or not called to serve at all, there was one thing they had to have. Fervent, sincere, continuous prayer was a requirement no matter who they were.

They had to develop and consistently maintain a close, deep, personal, prayer relationship with God. It was the only way to help them get through the difficult times. They had to pray their husbands through working, ministry and daily living. Husbands leaned on the prayers of their wives. In the Ministers and Deacons Wives Guild, I taught them how to support their husband through establishment of goals and objectives for their home and ministry. These women are different psychologically, spiritually and mentally from ordinary women in the church by virtue of their husband's position. Because I survived my marital problems, I counseled couples about how to look to the Lord and let Him be their guide. I mentioned to them how to come together in prayer. I even informed them some of the exact prayers I prayed.

"Lord, I'm just a child and I don't know what to do. Please take over this situation and guide this tongue of mine. Take control of it. I know you can do it. Lord help me. Take control of the situation. Teach me what I should say and do. Show it to me, Lord. Guide this tongue and I will obey."

Sometimes, I got tired of falling on my knees, but I had no other choice. That was the only way God showed me what my husband was going to do and how I was to respond.

He is not going to eat this food you prepared, but don't get upset.

"Yes Lord." Every time I said that, I felt the humility coming in me.

Treat him as the head.

There is nothing like turning your face to the wall and talking to Jesus for whatever you need.

Trinidad, Germany, London England, Africa, and Hawaii

God elevated me because I was obedient. Even in my elevation, there was testing. I was elevated and honored to travel overseas to help souls find salvation and teach them better ways of thinking, praying and living. I went there and represented our church. God blessed us and I was able to have conferences with the soldiers who were stationed and living in some of those places.

When I went to bed that night, some of the girls snuck into my apartment. Whatever they needed---undergarments, slips, food—if I had it, I gave it to them. A girl came to our hotel and knocked on my door. When I opened the door, she was apprehensive but bold with her request.

"I heard you gave my sister some undergarments and a slip. May I have some?"

"I don't have any more."

"Well, are you wearing any? I will take those."

My heart ripped in my chest. I went in the bathroom, pulled them off and gave them to her. Something that was such a minor thing to me was a life changing item to these young women who were my sisters and daughters in Christ on the other side of the world. God allowed me to recognize how blessed I was and how important it was to help everyone I could!

I was in Germany for a period and was able to be blessed by meeting the saints and praying them through their rough times. The apostle over there was able to join us in teaching the young people to love yourself and love your family. I was able to testify firsthand about tests that I suffered in my marriage and walk with God. He allowed me to experience a financial downfall. The leadership promised to pay my expenses if I went. God knew they would not honor their word. My husband, being a man of God, paid for my expenses and more.

Yes, there was elevation and suffering, but ultimately victory! Victory for me and for the precious saints of God in foreign lands. God blessed this girl from Alabama to step, walk, pray, live and tarry in foreign places. Each place has its own testimony on how God moved on someone's heart, through my footprint in their country.

Power of Prayer

During my son-in-law's first deployment, they were headed to the Mediterranean Ocean, in particular, Beirut, Lebanon. While underway, they noticed the weather getting warmer, the water becoming blue-er, and began wondering where they were headed. They ended up in the Caribbean Ocean, off the coast of Grenada. They weren't there very long before they began launching aircrafts. Later, they discovered the Russians were attempting take over the island and use it as a strategic stronghold against the United States of America.

On another occasion, while in the dining room preparing dinner for Bishop Hall, a great heavy burden came over me so much I couldn't eat. I began to scream. Bishop Hall looked at me, "Hattie what's wrong."

"I don't know why I'm feeling like this."

"Hattie, you know what to do."

I went into my secret closet and began to pray. "Lord what's going on? Take over whatever it is right now in the name of Jesus!"

The voice of the Lord said to me, *Vincent is in trouble, he is on a ship heading into a dangerous situation.*

Later, we were told the ship encountered a great storm with heavy waves while crossing the Atlantic Ocean. The ship was an aircraft carrier one of the largest vessels in the U.S. Navy, a floating Naval Air Station consisting of five to six thousand service members. You wouldn't believe how the waves and wind would affect its course. Nevertheless, the weather pressed upon the ship causing it to pitch and roll (rock), with heavy winds, waves and deep swells, but they made it to their destination safely. Praise God for the power of prayer!

Prayer – Landlord

At the time we were living in an apartment building, our landlord lived the next floor under me and William. I found out he always hurried to be at his apartment to hear me pray. So this one day, William was at work and I getting ready for my daily devotion to prayer, and I heard someone crying and knocking at my door. I asked who it was, it was the landlord. He said he had to come and tell me what was happening. He said my prayers was a blessing to him. I begin to talk to him about salvation. You never know how God is using you to bless someone. One of many times, Bishop Bonner put the church on a three-day fast. We went home, ready to eat after the fast and the Lord locked my mouth. I could not open it. God said, *"Don't eat. Not yet."*

After ten days, God released me to eat. Only God can give perfect peace because only He is perfect. There is no guile found in Him. You move when you are under the divine will of God. That flesh can say many things to you when going through three to ten days of fasting with no eating at all and just a little water. I cried as I sang the song. *Lead me, (by Doris Akers, 1953).* My mind was penetrated by those words.

Prayer Turned the Ambulance Around

A man staying in a Detroit hotel was having a heart attack. He called 911 for an ambulance. Somehow, God directed him to call our church for a minister to pray for him. I answered the phone, went to Bishop Bonner, mentioned to him what was happening and there were no ministers to pray for the man.

"Hattie! What's wrong with you? You know the power of prayer."

I returned to the caller and began to pray for him. The man called back the next night and told us he sent the ambulance back. He said to tell whoever prayed for him, thank you because God healed him! Let me tell you, God can do anything. All you got to do is believe Him.

A woman called and said, "The doctor said I got cancer and they want to operate immediately. I don't want to have the surgery because I'm afraid."

I talked to her and said, "Do you believe God can do it?"
"But I don't know how to believe! Can you pray with me?"

So after we prayed, I said, "When you go back to the doctor, go believing and tell the doctor you want an X-ray before you decide if you need the surgery. You will be surprised!"

"Alright, Mother Hall. I will." She called us back.
"Mother Hall! The doctor performed the surgery and remove a fibroid tumor. He could not find the cancer. They checked

me all over and said, "What happened? We don't see any sign of cancer."

Prayer is the key and faith unlocks the door. Prayer works. Only believe all things are possible with God!

CHAPTER 9
Family

As Godly parents, we have learned not to say, "Not my child!". As we have carried our cross, we knew our children also carried their crosses as preacher's kids (PK's). You would never know how deep sin affects the heart of a family until you are tested.

By Spring 1984, Lisa had graduated from high school. Being a dad of four girls, you pay attention to their every move. I watched my youngest daughter slowing finding interest in things we taught against. There were times in the middle of the night when I could quietly hear her playing worldly music from underneath her pillow. I thought telling her to turn off her radio was enough to let her know it wasn't right. Lisa was still fully active in the church with Sunday School, Bible class, singing in the choir, doing fundraisers, gospel skating and helping the seniors with their personal needs. Being a praying dad, I noticed her praise in God was changing.

They say the youngest is spoiled, yet Lisa was born 65. She always loved to be around and listen to people older than her. As godly parents, you learn how Satan always uses what is near to you, dear to you and familiar to you. This was the summer of 1987. As mom's normally do, I was cooking breakfast for Elder Hall when the phone rang. Lisa worked afternoons at AAA, so she was asleep.

"Good morning. This is Mrs. Smith calling with the keys to Lisa's new house."

"Excuse me. This is Mrs. Hattie *Hall*."

I repeated my last name to be sure this lady was calling the correct number. Mrs. Smith said it again that Lisa Hall's keys were ready. Knowing Satan is always working overtime, I immediately prayed within myself. It had to be the Lord that walked me upstairs to her room without grabbing and shaking her. Jesus kept me calm as I informed Lisa of this horrific call.

"Lord, this is my youngest child."

I don't remember all that went through my mind. At this time, Lisa was already 21 years old with a full-time job. She had been slowly venturing out of the church for some time. Lisa felt it would be respectful to purchase a home since the lifestyle she surprisingly chose would continually conflict with our dwelling place. That old slew footed Satan made her think she was doing right by purchasing her own house to live in sin.

It was our turn to receive the prayers of the saints. Some approached with prayers of empathy. Others approached with ridicule. We praise God that our Christian family was there for us. As a natural and spiritual mother, your kneeology is put to the test. I prayed for years for the Lord to bring our daughter back to us. It was 2000 when the Lord said to me, "You are not praying what I told you to pray". Immediately, I said, "Yes, Lord". Shortly after that, Lisa called to ask if she could bring some items to the house for storage. The Lord would not allow me to ask why. She was several months pregnant with her youngest daughter. Near the beginning of 2001, the Lord brought our youngest daughter back home to stay. Like the prodigal son, we welcomed our daughter home with open arms. All she could say was this was nobody but Jesus. The fullness of her testimony is yet to be heard. From that day forward, she has said, "I heard Jesus' voice and followed His clear instructions."

As Christian parents, we know all of our trials and tests are not the same, yet Satan has a hand somewhere. What he forgets is, "And we know that all things work together for good to them that love God, to them who are the called according to His purpose" (Romans 8:28).

As parents, you need to know who God blessed you to birth into this world. Satan has no dominion in your life. Fathers, mothers, grandparents, aunties and uncles – pray without ceasing for your families. The Lord is faithful!

CHAPTER 10
Serving with Bishop Henry IV and First Lady Davenport

To everything there is a season, and a time to every purpose under the heaven (Ecclesiastes 3:1).

We were blessed to know Pastor and Lady Davenport at the beginning of their ministry. God allowed us to bear witness to their growth in the Body of Christ. The Lord has birthed much endurance in their lives. Our relationship is special because we were able to teach and then learn from our new leaders in the gospel. Their humble spirits are full of joyful zeal for the Lord. We share the same fire for the Lord and for souls. Our goal is to grow the Kingdom which makes it easy to serve under their leadership.

Serving as the senior advisors throughout our church family was sanctioned by them both. They continue to show unity in their roles and have the solid foundation of the apostolic teachings. Them having a love relationship with our Lord and Savior pleases our historic father in the gospel, Bishop William Lee Bonner, as well as ourselves. As they continue with prayer as their number one foundation, it bridges connection to the youth and expands the outreach in the community.

It was surprising when Bishop and Lady Davenport made the decision to present the unorthodox gift to us of having our office expanded to accommodate our needs. Throughout these years of dedicated service, they have treated us with dignity, respect, love and honor. It wasn't just the physical blessings, but also the spiritual blessings. Serving amidst the leadership of unity with all leaders in the church is an example of a good Godhead. Our leaders have made sure that within the executive board, the trustees, the pastoral staff, cabinet and church members, there is love. This is the agape love that we have for one another. We pray for our Lord and Savior to continue in our lives as strong as the day of Pentecost. Hallelujah and glory to God!

CHAPTER 11
The Legacy of Bishop William and Mother Hattie Hall

God called us to serve. When we do all things with *love* then serving others is a joyful experience. Jesus said, *"if I be lifted up I will draw all men unto me."* We want everyone to come and know about Him. We encourage you to read about what you can do to be a blessing to the kingdom of God.

As every man hath received the gift, even so minister the same one to another, as good stewards of the manifold grace of God. If any man speak, let him speak as the oracles of God; If any man minister, let him do it as of the ability which God giveth: that God in all things may be glorified through Jesus Christ, to whom be praise and dominion forever and ever. Amen.
I Peter 4:10-11 KJV

Remember first of all to love God with all your heart, mind, soul and spirit. Excellence means to us that a life lived is lived out of habit because actually that is what excellence is, a habit. Not an act. Habit is when we're living this life and it is a life of positiveness. It's like driving an automobile. Excellence in habit is like an automatic transmission. With a standard transmission, you have to shift manually. But with an automatic transmission, all I have to do is step on the accelerator and the gears shift automatically. Making yourself do what is best is manually. If we do it automatically it is our character of excellence through our love and life of Jesus Christ.

Fifty-five plus years of prayer, fasting, suffering and sacrifice, totally committed to God. Faithful servants, never retired from serving God!

Appendix
The Gallery of Instruction

1. Spiritual Qualities of a Good Missionary
2. Guidelines For Tarrying with Souls
3. That Special Rib
4. The Importance of Communion
5. The Blessing Plan

SPIRITUAL QUALITIES OF A GOOD MISSIONARY

1. Obedient - 1 Peter 1:14
As obedient children, not fashioning yourselves according to the former lusts in your ignorance.

2. Humble - James 4:6
But he giveth more grace. Wherefore he saith, God resisteth the proud, but giveth grace unto the humble.

3. Patient - Luke 21:19
In your patience possess ye your souls.

Patient - 2 Timothy 2:24
And the servant of the Lord must not strive; but be gentle unto all men, apt to teach, patient

4. Not A Busybody - 1 Peter 4:15
But let none of you suffer as a murderer, or as a thief, or as an evildoer, or as a busybody in other men's matters.

Not A Busybody - 1 Timothy 5:13
And withal they learn to be idle, wandering about from house to house; and not only idle, but tattlers also and busybodies, speaking things which they ought not.

5. Teachers of Good Things - Titus 2:4, 5
Teach the young women to be sober, to love their husbands, to love their children, To be discreet, chaste, keepers at home, good, obedient to their own husbands, that the word of God be not blasphemed.

6. Of Good Report - Acts 16:2
Well reported of by the brethren that were at Lystra and Iconium.

7. Able to Follow Instructions - Proverbs 12:1
Whoso loveth instruction loveth knowledge: but he that hateth reproof is brutish.

8. Desire to Aid Sick and Needy - Acts 16:2
Which was well reported of by the brethren that were at Lystra and Iconium.

9. Supportive of Pastor and Leaders - Hebrews 13:17
Obey them that have the rule over you, and submit yourselves: for they watch for your souls, as they that must give account, that they may do it with joy, and not with grief: for that is unprofitable for you.

10. Knowledge of the Word - 2 Timothy 2:15
Study to shew thyself approved unto God, a workman that needeth not to be ashamed, rightly dividing the word of truth.

11. Love and Compassion for Souls - John 13:35
By this shall all men know that ye are my disciples, if ye have love one to another.

12. A Praying Saint - 1 Thessalonians 5:17
Pray without ceasing.

13. Seeks to Please God - Romans 12:1
I beseech you therefore, brethren, by the mercies of God, that ye present your bodies a living sacrifice, holy, acceptable unto God, which is your reasonable service.

14. Dresses as Becoming Holiness - 1 Timothy 2:9
In like manner also, that women adorn themselves in modest apparel, with shamefacedness and sobriety; not with braided hair, or gold, or pearls, or costly array;

Dresses as Becoming Holiness - 1 Peter 3:4
But let it be the hidden man of the heart, in that which is not corruptible, even the ornament of a meek and quiet spirit, which is in the sight of God of great price.

15. Faithful in Church Attendance - Matthew 25:21
His lord said unto him, Well done, thou good and faithful servant: thou hast been faithful over a few things, I will make thee ruler over many things: enter thou into the joy of thy lord.

Faithful in Church Attendance - Luke 12:42
And the Lord said, Who then is that faithful and wise steward, whom his lord shall make ruler over his household, to give them their portion of meat in due season?

16. Willing to Suffer Persecution - 2 Corinthians 12:10
Therefore I take pleasure in infirmities, in reproaches, in necessities, in persecutions, in distresses for Christ's sake: for when I am weak, then am I strong.

17. Knows Her Place In the Lord - 1 Corinthians 11:3
But I would have you know, that the head of every man is Christ; and the head of the woman is the man; and the head of Christ is God.

18. Fruit Bearer - John 15:5, 7, 8
I am the vine, ye are the branches: He that abideth in me, and I in him, the same bringeth forth much fruit: for without me ye can do nothing. If ye abide in me, and my words abide in you, ye shall ask what ye will, and it shall be done unto you. Herein is my Father glorified, that ye bear much fruit; so shall ye be my disciples.

19. Tithe and Offering Giver - Malachi 3:8-10
Will a man rob God? Yet ye have robbed me. But ye say, Wherein have we robbed thee? In tithes and offerings. Ye are cursed with a curse: for ye have robbed me, even this whole nation. Bring ye all the tithes into the storehouse, that there may be meat in mine house, and prove me now herewith, saith the Lord of hosts, if I will not open you the windows of

heaven, and pour you out a blessing, that there shall not be room enough to receive it.

20. Tithe and Offering Giver - Luke 6:38
Give, and it shall be given unto you; good measure, pressed down, and shaken together, and running over, shall men give into your bosom. For with the same measure that ye mete withal it shall be measured to you again.

We believe in all the teachings of the Apostles and Prophets. Jesus Christ Himself being the Chief Cornerstone. We believe it and are doers of the Word, not hearers only.

Guidelines for Tarrying with Souls

From The Desk of Bishop William L. Bonner

1. When tarrying with a seeker, the right frame of mind is essential. Therefore, it is required that a person pray for at least fifteen (15) minutes before tarrying with a seeker.

2. If two persons are tarrying with a seeker, only one of them should be speaking and that should be in a low tone of voice, never shouting in the ear of the seeker. The second person should be praying, never talking to the seeker until the first person has ceased to encourage the seeker.

3. Here is an example of an expression of encouragement, "Jesus is giving you the Holy Spirit today/tonight, just believe!" When a seeker feels the Spirit and it is evident to those tarrying with him/her, it is important that you don't get excited and begin to shout at the seeker. Keep encouraging them by saying; "The Holy Spirit is coming in, just yield to it, don't be afraid, just relax and let the Spirit have his way!" Others in the room should not rush to the seeker who is receiving the Holy Spirit and shout words of encouragement. It is too many voices and will be confusing to the seeker. Let everyone stay where they are and let the persons tarrying with that seeker remain with that seeker until he is filled.

4. Anyone with an offensive odor of the body or mouth should not tarry with seekers, but sit in the room and pray.

5. No one should lay hands on a seeker other than the minister.

6. When seekers are praising the Lord by saying, "Hallelujah" or "Thank you Jesus" and is in the spirit, do not change their praise.

7. No one should run from one seeker to another unless there is a shortage of workers.

8. The tarrying service is not for teaching doctrine or for long testimonies. The service is for people to receive the Holy Spirit. All exhortations should be short and encouraging to the seekers. It should encourage the seekers to receive the Holy Spirit; tell the seekers how to believe; how to have faith and release that faith.

9. If a seeker has been tarrying for an hour or an hour and a half on their knees, they should be encouraged to sit up.

10. Singing helps the seeker. After tarrying for an hour, the saints should sing while the seeker tarries. That would be a blessing. You should sing blood songs, faith songs, or songs of praise.

11. There should never be any expressions of disagreement or hostilities between saints in the tarrying service or in front of the seekers. Tarrying service is not the place for this kind of situation.

12. Never stop anyone from tarrying. They can gently be led to another room but never stop a soul from tarrying because you don't know how close they are to receiving the Holy Ghost.

NOTE: PLEASE PAY CLOSE ATTENTION TO THESE GUIDELINES.

That Special Rib
by Mother Hattie Hall – 2014

And the Lord God caused a deep sleep to fall upon Adam, and he slept: and he took one of his ribs, and closed up the flesh instead thereof; And the rib, which the Lord God had taken from man, made he a woman, and brought her unto the man. And Adam said, This is now bone of my bones, and flesh of my flesh: she shall be called Woman, because she was taken out of Man. (Genesis 2:21-23)

INTRODUCTION

You are "That Special Rib" taken out of your husband's side. You are bone of his bone, flesh of his flesh. God did not take that rib from him and disregard it; but God took him apart to put him back together - to create a Masterpiece! You are that rib or missing piece, that makes his life complete. Therefore, when fitly joined together, the "twain become one."

I. HIS PRAYER PARTNER

It's safe to say, that in most marriages, the wife prays more than the husband. She is usually the intercessor. Most women have a special ability - a spirit or constitution that cannot be easily broken. Therefore, she can get through to God faster.

When you go before the Lord in prayer, you should pray "for" your husband, not "on" him. When you pray "on" him, that signifies division and implies that he's your enemy. You're not his enemy. You are his own flesh, his partner. Pray for him; that God's will is done in his life and yours. Be his prayer partner, when he's praying, pray with him. When he's not praying, continue to pray.

One thing that is every important, don't pass judgment concerning your husband's relationship with the Lord. Even if his prayer life or Bible study is not up to par, don't harshly criticize him. But put forth a greater effort to encourage him to draw closer to God praying that his first love increases. Your husband needs your prayers. There are times when your sight is keener. Pray that God will open His eyes to see and ears to hear. Also, as the same time, pray that you will become attuned to God. Often times, when you point the finger at him, you should be saying: "It's me, it's me, it's me, oh Lord! Standing in the need of prayer."

Not only should you pray for your husband but pray for the marriage and the family as a whole. Just in case you didn't know it, the two of you are like an army: "One can chase a thousand, and two can put ten thousand to flight." In all marriages, disagreement and differences will emerge. But remember, you are fighting one another, to see whose will shall prevail. But you are wrestling against principalities and powers, the rulers of the darkness of this world. So there is always something to pray for and to pray against. The enemy is trying to destroy the God ordained institution of home and family. So you must be wise and pray that you stay married: "for marriage is ordained by God," Pray for peace, harmony and unity in the home. Be that warrior (soldier) whose weapon is prayer.

II. THE MOTIVATOR. NOT THE PUSHER

No man likes a nagging, pushy or contentious wife. It is better to dwell in the wilderness, than with a contentious and an angry woman. (Proverbs 21:19)

As coals are to burning coals, and wood to fire; so is a contentious man to kindle strife. (Proverbs 26:21)

A continual dropping in a very rainy day and a contentious woman are alike. (Proverbs 27:15)

Men hate to be fussed at or reprimanded, because it does nothing to stimulate them or foster growth. However, it deflates their egos. All men have egos and they want to keep them. Fussing at him only belittles and tarnishes his character. Most men have goals or dreams, but they often procrastinate and sometimes even become slothful. That's the time when you must encourage and stimulate him. This calls for wisdom. You should know him like a book. So, study him. Know his likes and dislikes, his moods, and what turns him on and off. Know how, where and when to approach him. Learn to say the right thing at the right time.

A word fitly spoken is like apples of gold in pictures of silver. (Proverbs 25:11)

Keep me as the apple of the eye, hide me under the shadow of thy wings (Psalms 17:8)

Learn to compliment him. Even if it seems like everything he does is wrong, find something. Try saying: "Honey, you look nice, or I love the way you do this or that." And when nothing else works, say that very thing you constantly love to hear yourself, "I Love you." A husband needs to know that his wife is in his corner. With all the pressure on him today, he too needs constant encouragement, tell him: "Honey, everything is going to be okay; we can make it." Marriage is more than a full-time job; in fact you have to put in more overtime than regular working hours. Marriage is a lot of give and take, more give than take. And women usually do most of the giving. Even if it seems that you never receive, your work and self-sacrifice will pay off. By giving and giving, sooner or later the husband is going to take another look; and your love will motivate him. In order to motivate someone, you have to be motivated yourself. Even though you play many roses, as wife, mother, you still need space for you to grow as an individual. Discover your gifts, talents, and skills. Then put them to work. Busy yourself, your mind must be active. (Not active in someone else's matters (busy body), but actively working for God). While working with and beside your husband, do something that is self-fulfilling or to build your self-esteem. Perhaps it's teaching Sunday School, visiting the sick, helping the needy, or a hobby or even a career. In order to help him, you must have something to offer. Every wife should strive to be well-rounded. Eager to learn, to listen and to grow to be that "virtuous woman" so that "her husband is known in the gates, when he sitteth among the elders of the land. (Proverbs 31:23)

III. THE BACKBONE

Whether he admits it or not, your husband leans on you for support. He wants to be able to count on you when no one else seems to understand. If he's involved in a work for Christ (as a deacon, minister, etc...) don't make comments such as "I didn't want to marry a preacher or deacon." You did, even though you didn't realize it at the time. Remember, you married him for "better or worse." Did you ask for a husband? Did you get one? Well, accept him totally; what he is, and what he's to become. If you refuse to accept the call of his life, you are telling the Lord you don't' want His will to be done. Don't try to shape him to fit your mold. Let the potter shape the clay. You can't change anybody. If he needs to be broken, let God do it. The Lord knows him better than you. He, (the Lord) will break him in the right place; you won't.

By accepting the role, you are willing to do whatever you can to support him so that he can be God's special vessel. Not only are you to support him in church, but in general. Support his goals and aspirations. That Backbone ("You") can either help support, make or break him. Which have you chosen to do? Electing to help make him, you too will realize personal fulfillment, and be wonderfully blessed.

IV. HIS COMRADE

The bottom line is - be his best friend (second to Christ). Laugh with him, enjoy his company. Even be his "buddy." Remember when the two of you used to talk for hours on end? Do you still talk with one another? Or is it "at" one another or "through" the kids? Positive communication is a must. Don't just talk, but listen to one another. Also, do things (for fun) on a regular basis. Break away from the job, kids and other responsibilities. Go out for dessert, a drive, and even steal away or elope for a while and go on vacations. Enjoy one another. It's important that you date one another. In fact, this is the ideal time to do it. Above all, be friends! For "true friends are like gold precious and rare. It's hard to find a piece of gold; harder to find is a real friend." Woman was made from the rib of man; she was not created from his head to top him, nor from his feet to be stepped upon. She was made from his side to be equal to him. From beneath his arm to be protected by him, hear his heart to be loved by him.

This is a word-by-word transcript taken directly from
The Importance of Communion
taught by Bishop William G. Hall
September 14, 2017

The Importance of Communion

The definition of Communion, according to Webster's Dictionary: It is a group of Christians professing the same faith and practicing the same rites. Now it becomes different in a sense when we use the word HOLY in front of it. Instead of just Communion, it makes a difference to say Holy Communion, is that right?

Now when we define Holy Communion according to Webster's Dictionary: It is many or various Christian rites in which bread and wine are consecrated and received as the Body and Blood of Jesus or as symbols of them. It's actually a sacrament of the Lord's Supper. So when we use the word Communion or Holy Communion, the Lord's Supper means the same.

The Communion service, Dear Hearts, Listen to me good. The Communion Service is one of the most important services of the church because we must realize that when we are taking communion, it is two things. It is both a memorial, because I believe Jesus told us to do this in remembrance of him and it is a celebration which means we show his death until he comes. That's why it's so important.

Now, The Lord's Supper or Holy Communion, the First Communion was served in the Book of Genesis 14:18 where Melchizedek, the Priest of the Most High God gave First Communion to our father, Abraham and you know what it consisted of? Bread and wine. Alright it says here: Christ being a High Priest after the Order of Melchizedek evidently administered the same in the book of Hebrews 7:17.

Now Dear Hearts, water and grape juice are modern substitutes that have been invented by the formal church of today in which many who have never been regenerated, in other words, born again or the Spirit. Now I would like to say also in passing, when it comes to Holy Communion as to the time, place or frequency of this ordinance, the scripture does not teach. Now it being an ordinance, I want to define the word Ordinance. An ordinance is just like a direction or a command of an authoritative nature. In other words that which is held to be a decree of faith of a Deity. So this ordinance which it is, is not a sacrament as taught by some. Conveying effectual grace to the soul and imparting spiritual life but - but is always the other side of the coin. But the divinely appointed ordinances as a means of grace, the importance must not be undervalued - talking about Holy Communion - never undervalued.

The question has been raised, you know what it is? Should we eat the literal bread and drink of the literal wine? Or it says here, should we just by faith partake of it spiritually? Listen to me closely. Just by faith partake of it spiritually says something. Others teach that we should take water instead of wine, etc. While others teach it is only a symbol to be practiced by the church according to their pleasure. Guess what? Both of them were wrong. Both of the teachings that I just gave to you are wrong. And I'm going to state why. I'm reading a whole lot because it is better for me to read it than to try to remember it. The bread and wine of The Lord's Supper are not mere symbols, types or shadows. The bread and the wine are legitimate. You know what legitimacy is? Credentialed. They are representatives of the broken body and the shed blood of our Lord Jesus Christ. They are witnesses to testify of that which has happened on purpose making for us reconciliation unto God. Our partaking of the same is our work. Making our faith whole in the stripes, thorn crowned head, pierced side and broken body, My Lord, then something else comes up. Who should take it? Guess who should take it? I want to state something that Paul stated. Paul said, as oft as you do it, you do show forth the Lord's death until he comes, which is in 1 Corinthians 11:26. Jesus said, Drink ye all of it. Again Paul said, whosoever eateth and drinketh unworthily of the cup of the Lord eateth and drinketh damnation to himself, not discerning the Lord's body. Not discerning signifies that there is a lack of inspired wisdom to have discernment. Being capable of discerning signifies acute sureness, shrewdness, the wise shall understand.

Dear Hearts, spiritually speaking, you can neither eat nor drink unworthily. You can eat the little bread and drink the little wine not being worthy or rather not having an inspired revelation of God. To drink of the spiritual rock and to eat of the spiritual loaf, you must be made worthy by the Father of

Lights. Revelation says, there is no variableness, neither a shadow of turning for in revelation you are being made partakers of His divine nature.

Isn't that something? Just like you are partakers of your human parents' nature, we become partakers of Jesus Christ's divine nature. So whosoever drinketh this cup of the Lord with no consecrated surrendering in their hearts to suffer with him, in suffering of sacrifice unto death, eats and drinks of the cup of the Lord unworthily. When Jesus went forth to drink of the Cup of Suffering he said, my soul is exceedingly sorrowful, even unto death. He told the disciples, tarry ye here and watch with me. His soul was in pain and sorrow. He had come to the place of drinking the bitter taste of that cup of suffering. He went a little farther and fell on his face and prayed, saying, "Oh my father, if it be possible, let this cup pass from me. Nevertheless, not as I will but as thy will. My Father, if this cup may not pass away from me except I drink it, thy will be done."

You know there is something even about the will of the human being. God created man. He really, as Paul says, the first man Adam was created a living soul. So man is actually a soul that is in a body and he has a spirit. Now the soul is actually the core of the man. And in that soul, I think it has about three entities. There is the thinking part. There is the will. And then there is the emotions. Note: God was manifested in the flesh. He became a human being. And as the Son of God note what he said. He wanted his will to be done and his will was not to drink of the bitter cup. But it was not the Father's will so whose will is best? That's why we must also surrender and say, not my will but as thou will. Now Jesus took bread and he blessed it. Note now: Watch it. Before he even started passing it out, he blessed it. He blessed it before he broke it. What is the significance of that? Alright I would say, I think Paul gave us an understanding of it in 1 Corinthians 10 where it says the cup of blessings which we bless is it not the Communion of the Blood of Christ? The bread which we break is it not the Communion of the Body of Christ? You see, Dear Hearts, once the man of God blesses that table, and you come up to partake of it, you are no longer taking bread and wine. Because I know a lot of times I watch some people and they come up, since it's the Body of Jesus Christ, his actual Body we should even be careful of how we handle it. I try to be so careful of when I pick it up, I want to make sure that none drops from my hands. Because if it drops on the floor just like I have watched those who prepare Communion, unless that body now, because it is the body now it has been blessed, unless it hits the floor, we should never take it off the altar because it has fell from the tray and put it on the cart. We have in mind of doing what? Throwing it away. YOU DON'T TREAT THE BODY OF THE LORD JESUS CHRIST THAT WAY! Isn't that right? THANK YOU, JESUS!

Alright so Jesus took bread and blessed it and brake it and gave it to the disciples and said, now this is what Jesus said. "Take, eat, this is my body." And - now and is a conjunction from my understanding. I've been out of school for years but I always remember and is a conjunction. And what does a conjunction do? Connects. Hallelujah! It connects.

He took the cup and gave thanks and gave it to them saying, "Drink ye all of it!" Listen to what he says. "For this is my blood of the New Testament.? The songwriter picked it up and said: What can wash away my sins? Nothing but the Blood of Jesus. What can make me whole again? Nothing but the Blood of Jesus. I like that song that our Establishmentarian wrote and as I was singing it in my meditations, I realized that he spoke in that song of the broken body and the shed blood. It says: Blessed Jesus thou has saved me. Thou has filled my heart with joy. In thy name I have salvation. Through thy precious cleansing blood. Cleansing blood. Nothing can wash away my sins. Nothing but the blood of Jesus.

Now for him to mention the bread, he says: Thou art God my Holy Father. Bread of life thou art to me. Living water from the fountain. Thou hast given me liberty. Oh Lord I love you! And Jesus said, "Drink ye all of it. For this is my blood of the New Testament which is shed for many for the remission of sins." Listen to what John says when he saw him walking on the Sea of Galilee. He said Behold! In other words, look here comes the Lamb of God that cometh not to cover man's sin, but to take it away for the remission of sins. Listen Dear Hearts, we dare not turn away from our testimony of consecration. We also dare not refuse to partake. What? We dare not also refuse to take. If we refuse to pledge ourselves in consecration by our testimony partaking of his broken body and shed blood, guess what? We thereby take ourselves off of the Altar of Sacrifice. Now that act makes us unworthy of the Altar of Incense. We cannot be partakers of the Altar of Incense and not be consecrated upon the Altar of Sacrifice. On the Altar of

Sacrifice we will yield daily on and at the Altar of Incense we are sending sweet praises and thanksgiving unto God. And drinking of His inspiring glory. Listen to the following words of the poet. That express: Dying with Jesus by death reckoned mind. Living with Jesus a new life divine. Looking to Jesus till glory doth shine. Moment by moment oh Lord I am thine.

I love that song that says:
I am thine Oh Lord,
And I've heard thy voice
And it told thy love to me.
But I long to rise in the arms of faith
And be closer drawn to thee.
I like that second verse that says:
Consecrate me now to thy service Lord
By thy power of grace divine.
Let my soul, my very soul look up with a steadfast hope
And my will be lost in thine.

Here again, I'm going to repeat a scripture. Paul says: "For I have received of the Lord that which also I deliver unto you that the Lord Jesus the same night in which he was betrayed took the bread and when he had given thanks, brake it and said, take eat, this is my body it is broken for you. This do in remembrance of me. After the same manner also he took the cup and supped and said this is the New Testament in my blood, this do ye as oft as ye drink it, in remembrance of me. For as often as ye eat this bread and drink of this cup you do show the Lord's death until he come. Wherefore, whosoever shall eat this bread and drink of this cup unworthily shall be guilty of the blood and the body of the Lord. He that endureth to the end, the same shall be saved." Now they who consecrate themselves in the fellowship of his suffering are going to endure. To reap the crown of life, they must endure until the end. The cup of wine that we bless and partake of is our pledge of purity and devotion to the cup of suffering of our Lord Jesus.

Here again, the cup which we bless is it not the communion of the Body of Christ. Now it also says here, "We being many are one bread and one body. For we are all partakers of that one bread." You remember in the Bible, when the two sons of Zebedee with their mother came to Jesus, worshipping and desiring a certain thing of him. He answered them and said, "You know not what you ask. Are you able to drink of the cup that I shall drink of and to be baptized with the baptism that I am baptized with? They said, we are able. He said to them, ye shall indeed drink of my cup and be baptized with the baptism that I am baptized with. Now we all recognize that to be the cup of suffering which he prayed to the Father might pass if it be possible. It was not possible, so he drank of it.

The baptism that he refers to saying that I am baptized with is the Pentecostal Baptism of the Holy Ghost. Now all through the ages there has been a custom for men to pledge their loyalty and to consecrate themselves in the wine cup. In some ancient orders they drank the wine and wrote their names in the blood. From that pledge there was no turning back. When you went to the Altar of Repentance and dedicated yourself to God you also dedicated yourselves to his broken body and shed blood. When you partook of that bread and that cup of wine, you consecrated yourself in fellowship to partake of the suffering of Christ. If you did not make that consecration then you are guilty of the body and blood of the Lord. Wherefore whosoever shall eat this bread and drink of this cup of the Lord unworthily shall be guilty of the body and the blood of the Lord. But let a man examine himself and so let him eat of that bread and drink of that cup, for he that eateth and drinketh unworthily eateth and drinketh damnation unto himself not discerning the Lord's body.

In my conclusion, if you dare refuse to eat and drink, you by so doing refuse to suffer with him. Therefore, you will not be counted worthy to reign with him. If you refuse because you are unworthy, you heap damnation unto yourself. If you partake unworthily, you simply eat and drink damnation unto yourself. The only thing that you can do to escape damnation is to examine yourselves before God in humble, penitent, prayerful consecration and surrender to suffer with him. Then you can eat and not drink damnation unto yourselves. I want you to note two things. There are two main reasons why we take Communion. Can anyone tell me? You got it right but I would like for you to put it in order. I don't like to put two before one. We do it first of all in remembrance of him. I really don't want any questions because I went to the hospital one time to see a sister that was very sick. I mean she was sick to death. I took her Communion. She refused to take it. She said, "I am too sick to take Communion." So when I went back and told the pastor about it, he said, "Do you know what she did?" What pastor?" "She refused her healing." With the broken body it is for your healing. With the cup where he shed his blood, it is for your cleansing. Did not I say, What can wash away my sin? Nothing but the Blood of Jesus.

141

So in partaking, don't forget, when you partake its for your healing and for your cleansing. Now Pastor, I'm going to let you answer the questions. No you are doing a great job Bishop! We are a team. I like you on my team. And I like to be on your team.

Answering the Question "Can anyone tell me the two main reasons why we take communion?"

It's an ordinance. It's one of the ordinances in the church. But in taking Communion, the specific answer would be that we take it like he said. This do in remembrance of me. And also to show his death until he comes. Jesus, I'll never forget what you've done for me. Hallelujah! So when I take that body, after it's blessed, that's so meaningful. After it is blessed. I'm going to ask a question then I'm going to answer it. Why do you think that we are careful after everybody has taken Communion, sometimes some of the body is left. We are careful not to throw that in the garbage because it has not ceased to be the broken body. Once it's blessed, it's the holy broken body, even after you get through it doesn't cease to be. So we should be careful how we do it. So we call ourselves doing it the Apostolic way. Now I'm going to say this and then I'm going to have another class. Believe it or not, Dear Hearts, who does God really glory in? Let me start from the bottom.

Where is a woman's glory?
Her hair.
What is a man's glory?
The woman.

What is God's glory?

The man. He glories in a man. Not Christ. I'm going to tell you why He glories in a man. Do you not know it is an insult to God for a man He has created male, masculine to get up on TV and say, "I'm a woman trapped in a man's body." I need to take my belt off and get started. I shouldn't have said that, should it. But do you all see where I'm coming from? So it is an insult to God. I created you a man. I want you to be a man. Act like a man. And conduct yourself like a man. And I don't think a man as a man might be called a man if he strikes his wife. I'm through. In fact he has to be careful not to be bitter against her. Oh oh! Ouch! I even have to watch that. Now they got on Moses' nerves. Sometimes you can have a little misunderstanding but we don't let that become detrimental to us, we get that straightened out.

A question was asked: There are times in our lives when we have done something wrong and we do not feel worthy to take Holy Communion, did we sin? I think you do wrong if you don't take Communion. Isn't the blood for cleansing? Don't let the devil fool you and tell you, oh, I've done something wrong and I'm not going to take it. That's what it's for. And once it's blessed, it is the broken body of Jesus Christ and his shed blood. And I don't know of anything that can cleanse a person from their sin like the Blood of Jesus can. So, I would say they should take communion.

Am I in the book pastor? This is teamwork. Communion is the New Covenant. (Bishop Davenport Takes Over the

Remaining Portion of the Class.) Let's water the seed of that Word right now with praise and worship of Jesus Christ.

He has served under Bishop Bonner for so many years and now that God has taken Bishop Bonner to heaven, glory he is working with me and I appreciate him so very much. One more time, let's praise God for Bishop Hall.

The Blessing Plan

Deuteronomy 28:1-14

1. And it shall come to pass, if thou shalt hearken diligently unto the voice of the Lord thy God, to observe and to do all his commandments which I command thee this day, that the Lord thy God will set thee on high above all nations of the earth:

2 And all these blessings shall come on thee, and overtake thee, if thou shalt hearken unto the voice of the Lord thy God.

3 Blessed shalt thou be in the city, and blessed shalt thou be in the field.

4 Blessed shall be the fruit of thy body, and the fruit of thy ground, and the fruit of thy cattle, the increase of thy kine, and the flocks of thy sheep.

5 Blessed shall be thy basket and thy store.

6 Blessed shalt thou be when thou comest in, and blessed shalt thou be when thou goest out.

7 The Lord shall cause thine enemies that rise up against thee to be smitten before thy face: they shall come out against thee one way, and flee before thee seven ways.

8 The Lord shall command the blessing upon thee in thy storehouses, and in all that thou settest thine hand unto; and he shall bless thee in the land which the Lord thy God giveth thee.

9 The Lord shall establish thee an holy people unto himself, as he hath sworn unto thee, if thou shalt keep the commandments of the Lord thy God, and walk in his ways.

10 And all people of the earth shall see that thou art called by the name of the Lord; and they shall be afraid of thee.

11 And the Lord shall make thee plenteous in goods, in the fruit of thy body, and in the fruit of thy cattle, and in the fruit of thy ground, in the land which the Lord sware unto thy fathers to give thee.

12 The Lord shall open unto thee his good treasure, the heaven to give the rain unto thy land in his season, and to bless all the work of thine hand: and thou shalt lend unto many nations, and thou shalt not borrow.

13 And the Lord shall make thee the head, and not the tail; and thou shalt be above only, and thou shalt not be beneath; if that thou hearken unto the commandments of the Lord thy God, which I command thee this day, to observe and to do them:

14 Thou shalt not go aside from any of the words which I command thee this day, to the right hand, or to the left, to go after other gods to serve them.

List of Achievements for William and Hattie Hall

Mother Hattie is an inductee in:

- The Mother Carrie Lawson Hall of Fame
- The Missionary Department Hall of Fame
- The Sisterhood Department Hall of Fame
- The Ministers and Deacons Wives Guild Hall of Fame

Degree:

"Doctor of Divinity" from Sacramento Theological Seminary and Bible College, November 2009

Certificates:

- "Certificate of Honor" Ministers/Deacons Wives Guild, November 1999
- "Continuing Education - The Mission/Focused Church" from W.L. Bonner College, July 2007
- "Certificate of Appreciation for Love Expression" (Bishop Bonner 2008 Birthday Celebration)
- "Certificate of Excellence" from Berea School of Theology, September 2003
- "Certificate of Appreciation as a Facilitator"- Church of Our Lord Jesus Christ, August 2005
- "Diplomat Christian Teaching Certificate" from Sacramento Theological Seminary, September 2008 – September 2009
- "Letter from the White House" from President Obama for her 80th birthday celebration - 2011

Bishop William Hall:

- "District Elder Credential" (The Church of Our Lord Jesus Christ of the Apostolic Faith, Inc. Headquarters: New York, New York) August 2002
- "Bishop Credential" – July 2007 (The Church of Our Lord Jesus Christ of the Apostolic Faith, Inc. Headquarters: New York, New York)
- "Certificate of Appreciation for 49 years of Sacrificial Service as Assistant Pastor" (Solomon's Temple) – June 2010
- "Doctor of Divinity Honorary Degree" from Sacramento Theological Seminary and Bible College, May 2009
- "Berea School of Theology First Alumni Seminar" certificate award – July 2002
- "Berea School of Theology Certificate of Completion" – January 2004

Bishop William and Mother Hattie Hall:

- "Certificate of Appreciation Caregivers Ministry Network" (Chosen Generations Community Center- Detroit, Michigan) – August 2003
- "State of Michigan Resolution" special tribute from Phil Cavanagh, State Representative 10th District (2011)
- "Special Tribute" from Virgil Smith, Senate Senator District 4 - Detroit (Celebrating 52 years servicing the Lord) July 2014

Testimonials

Elder Vincent Geter, Sr.

"And the earth was without form, and void; and darkness was upon the face of the deep. And the Spirit of God moved upon the face of the waters… And God said…....In the image of God created He him, male and female created He them." (Genesis 1:1, 26)

For whom He did foreknow, He also did predestinate to be conformed to the image of His Son, that He might be the firstborn among many brethren. Moreover whom He did predestinate, them He also called: and whom He called, them He also justified: and whom He justified, them He also glorified. What shall we then say to these things? If God be for us, who can be against us? (Romans 8:29-31)

We all were known by God before the beginning of time. My mother-in law, Hattie Hall, was designed, fashioned, called, and purposed to perform God's work in this world. Webster's New World Dictionary defines virtue as good qualities, great qualities, and God-like qualities that are inherent within an individual of impeccable character. Impeccability is that which is flawless, immaculate, without blemish, untainted, and unspotted. While these qualities represent our Lord Jesus Christ, He expects His children to grow and progress in a manner that reflects many, if not all of His attributes.

With that said, let me introduce you to Hattie Hall. "Mother Hall" is how she's known; a soldier on the battlefield for the Lord; a soul winner, a mercy show-er, hospitable, loving, and forgiving is what she shows. She is also a wife, a mother, a teacher, an example, and the personification, embodiment, and portrait that exemplifies holy women of God. Mother Hall is a worker, laborious, productive, spiritual; a Spirit-filled leader. She's a builder, not of structures, buildings, or edifices, but of the souls of men, women, and children. Many, near and far were affected by this woman's inner force that flowed outwardly through her words, presence, actions, and God-like behavior. We salute you, we praise God for you; we praise God for your life, your work, and your legacy!

"Favour is deceitful, and beauty is vain: but a woman that feareth the Lord, she shall be praised. Give her of the fruit of her hands; and let her own works praise her in the gates. (Proverbs 31: 30-31)

Gerald Young

How well do I remember in the early 60s. I was only six years old when my mother joined Solomon's Temple. At that time, it was called (Church Of Our Lord Jesus Christ) on Halleck and Dequindre - the only church I ever remember attending. We lived two blocks from the church. I remember when Bishop Hall, at that time he was Minister Hall, would bring bread and doughnuts by our home at the end of the day, when he would get off from his job at A & P grocery store. He could not stand for them to throw the bread and doughnuts away so he would give them to the saints at the church.

I remember very well how I loved listening to Bishop Hall preach during my younger years. He made the word of God very easy to understand. I always thought he was the pastor at that time. Pastor Bonner was in New York a lot. In my early teens I decided I wanted to be saved so I got baptized and started tarrying for the gift of the Holy Ghost. At that time there were many saints tarrying with souls at the altar. I only wanted Mother Hall to tarry with me. I knew every time she would kneel and pray next to me, I would feel the anointing of God that was on her. Also, I remember when I was six years old, Mother Hall tarrying with my mother (Elnora Young) and grandmother (Dollie Minniefee) later on. After receiving the precious gift of the Holy Ghost at 18 years of age, six years later on May 10, 1980, I married Bishop and Mother Hall's second oldest daughter, my love, Kim. From our union, our daughter Keela and son William were born. I named William after his grandfather, Bishop William Hall.

Wilbert Baber

Just like my family, there are no stepchildren. I feel like my in-laws are more of a second set of parents. I know that JESUS is the only perfect man that walked the earth, but Bishop and Mother Hall are running a close second in my eyes. What makes that so is how they could have a discernment of something and yet it is taken to GOD in prayer. GOD and FAMILY are everything!

Marshay

When I think of my grandmother, the first word that comes to mind is WARRIOR. Yes, she is the mother of four beautiful girls, but she is a mother to all who cross her path. She is a teacher, comforter, and prayer warrior. But most of all she shows love unconditionally. My grandmother has instilled in me all of her attributes that makes her the person she is today. I carry these same attributes with me wherever I go and to whomever I encounter. Who can ask for more than that from their grandmother? Luv ya much!

Keela Young

Heart of gold, full of life, compassion, caring, loving, giving, amazing, humble, patient, conservative, hilarious, wisdom, woman of God. These are only a few words of what my grandmother means to me. She is the heartbeat of this family - the blood pumping in our veins. She gives me life and words of encouragement. When I tell you she has a true heart of gold-it is the total truth. When she gives, she always says, "Oh I wish I had more" and my response is "Ummmmmm, what do you mean this is good enough ma'am". Oh and her funny side is one of the best things I love about my grandmother. We can joke and laugh all day. Overall, there are not enough words to say how awesome she is in my life. God has made a one true angel.

William Young

There's some pretty cool grandparents out there but sorry God blessed me with the best of them all. No matter what has happened in my life or the bad decisions I've made, they have always loved me unconditionally. Not once have my grandparents judged me. They are a true example of what love is. I know without the prayers of my grandmother I couldn't have made it this far in life. She's a true definition of a prayer warrior. I thank God for her. The smile that she makes when she sees me is priceless. Her knowledge and wisdom are crazy. She knows when something is wrong... it's like she was born with a sixth sense, her spiritual sense. She will detect the problem, stare at you, send up a prayer and smile all without saying a word. And she's clever because whenever my grandad would slip me some cash, she would follow right behind and give me double sometimes triple and wink as if to say don't tell your grandfather.

My grandparents are like real life superheroes...a dynamic duo that can't be messed with, possessing real life superpowers. I don't know how this is even possible but for those who don't know my grandad is pretty well seasoned in age but will still put any young man on their butt. Don't believe me, ask his oldest grandson. Strength, wisdom, cleverness, faith and prayer are just some of the many powers that God has blessed them with but the one that stands out the most is the power of love... Unconditional love... This duo is better than Batman and Robin, Michelle and Barack because they are one... One with God... and with God all things are possible... I'm his chip off the old block...Future Mandinga Warrior... Look at him and you'll see me... That's where I got my bow legs and good looks from...Love you guys until the end... I hope I'll be able to come close to be just as great as you.

Vincent Geter, Jr.

My Grandmother. First of all, I want to say I LOVE YOU from the bottom of my heart. I will never forget how you always prayed for me, even when I thought I didn't need it. I know your prayers were answered, because no matter what obstacles I had throughout my life I was able to overcome them. Another thing that I will never forget is how much power your voice carries. Seeing you tell a stranger (in the calmest voice) to pull his pants up to his waist, like a grown man, shocked me. What shocked me was how he listened and said yes ma'am with a positive attitude. That let me know how strong my grandmother is. When I speak to others about her, I let them know that she has a sweet and calm voice, but it carries a lot of strength and power. Three words that describe her in my eyes are strong-minded, truthful and loving. More wives, mothers and grandmothers should strive to be more like her. I am thankful to have her as a grandmother. I LOVE YOU.

Sherrell Delaney-Baber

My grandmother is "MINESSS" as I would say to myself even though I grew up having to share her love. She has always seemed like an angel to me, a person on this earth who could do no wrong. A servant of God with love to give from her own heart. As a young girl, I would watch her. I watched her as a wife, mother, teacher, leader and child of God. I admire her devotion, in my eyes she always gives her all. It seemed like God just gave her the strength to "do it all" and not feel the load of the day's work until all was done. I love that I can

154

talk to her about anything with openness far from judgment. Sometimes she shares stories with me about her past growing up in the south. Not only do I get mini family lessons, but it helps me understand how God molded her into the woman she is today. To be like her, I also bought my own class ring similar to her design, once I graduated college; she inspired me. With inspiration also came encouragement. My grandfather knows how to make a person feel they can be the best they can be which drives me to do so. His intelligence challenges me but yet he does not intimidate. My grandfather always reminds me of the person I am, could and should be. I appreciate all of his support and enthusiasm toward the journeys I have taken in life. From listening to me practice, playing the violin to going away to college, his support always shifted but never went away. I love him and I thank God for keeping him. I'm thankful for the man he is and still strives to be; he is a role model. Both of my grandparents have been there for me and my family in many ways. It doesn't matter if I am far away or near, my grandfather and grandmother have both been supportive every step of the way. I truly love them for that. I'm blessed to have both grandparents growing up. Their energy is a warmth and fulfillment I carry in my heart.

Jolenia Baber

My grandmother, the most inspirational woman I know, is the greatest role model of a grandmother you could ever have. She does so much, not just for herself, but for others too. She has the sweetest four daughters that mean the world to her. My mother, the youngest, is always looking out for her to make sure she is doing great. My grandmother has known tons of people that love her and would sacrifice lots just to make her day. The way she treats me is just wonderful. She takes care of me like I'm her own daughter. She calls me whenever she feels like she needs to or just to say hello, I LOVE that about her. Sometimes when my mother, grandmother and I go shopping to a store like Burlington, she always is willing to buy me a skirt or two for church. Every time she asks me that, I always get a little excited, but then I think, she already does so much for me. She is always looking out for me with a big smile. Yes, there are times when she is very serious, but it's only for the good of everyone. Whenever she needs help, I am there for her so she won't have any troubles. When I make her happy it's like seeing a shooting star and your wish came true. My grandmother likes to stay updated with my life whenever she has the time. I tell her what's up and the nice or not so nice details that went down. Of course, she listens and cares all the time. When my grandfather takes us three out to dinner, she makes sure I can get what I want and get very full off of it. She is always staying in the word of God. My grandmother is so quickly willing to sacrifice to go to church every time they have an event or service. As old as she is, I still call her young, that is a lot of weight put on her. I look up to her so much, and she does all of this awesomeness through God and I thank him for this miracle that He has blessed me with. I absolutely LOVE my grandmother and I hope she has an even longer life.

Josiah

My Great-Grandmother is a very inspiring and wonderful woman. She touches people's lives without even realizing it. Over the 18 years of my life, she has helped and advised me. I love her very much for it!

Kaelin

My grandparents are so loving to me and helpful. They are always helping out with my fundraisers at school and dance. I am so grateful that I am their great-granddaughter and they are my great-grandparents.

Nina Merie

You are an awesome great-grandma! I love you so much and you have been there for your family. That is one thing that makes you awesome!

Malakhai

I love my great-grandmother so much and she loves me back!

Fannie Jackson (Mother Hattie Hall's sister)

I can truly say ever since the Lord called her for service, she has worked tremendously in winning souls for Jesus Christ. In the late years of her life, she has not given up yet. May the peace of God be with us and cover us richly.

Harry Jackson (Mother Hattie Hall's brother)

My remembrance of my sister Hattie Jackson goes back to the 1940's. She is an older sister to me. Being the youngest in the house, my job was to listen and learn from the rest. During those years, I remember hearing my mother's voice in prayer daily. It was from my mother that Hattie learned to pray. I also listened to the prayers of my sister Hattie. Her prayers helped to form my views on prayer. Thank you, big sister and brother-in-law, for your praying spirit. Blessings to both of you from your youngest brother and brother-in-law.

Rodney U. Bellamy

Thank you for giving me the opportunity to share my memory of the marriage and lives of my Uncle William Hall and Aunt Hattie Hall. I'd like to share how they impacted my childhood and my adult life. I am Rodney U. Bellamy, one of 52 cousins, nieces and nephews in our large, tightly connected family. Typically, I choose to explain our bloodline.

I am the youngest of two (2) boys born to Ulysses Bellamy, Jr. and Ruth Mae Baldwin Jackson Bellamy. My mother Ruth was the younger sister to my aunt Hattie Baldwin Jackson Hall. Our mother & aunt were two of 12 surviving children out of 24 offspring born to Peter Jackson and Hattie Baldwin Jackson. We refer to our overall family as Baldwin and consistently celebrate our collective love and are thankful for where and what God has brought us through. A portion of my early childhood was spent with my older brother, living with the Halls and our cousins Delphine, Kim, Janese, and

Sherlenia. I don't really recall living with my uncle, aunt, and "cousins"…I remember the closeness of living with "sisters". I've always appreciated our relationships.

My mother guided our early spiritual growth in the Church of Our Lord Jesus Christ (later renamed Solomon's Temple) with her sister Hattie, where her brother-in-law William served as Assistant Pastor. Even after we grew our relationship with God in another church, and my mother passed away, we maintained our close bonds. In my totally adult years, during one of the most challenging periods of my life, my marriage was deteriorating. I sought out TRUE, God-inspired counsel for direction, guidance, and discipline. I sat in the Halls' kitchen, where I used to spend my childhood having meals and receiving their God-inspired wisdom. And now, as my Aunt Hattie served me food as a grown man, I still sit in their kitchen and received their wisdom. While I had my own perception of how perfect "courting" and marriage is supposed to be, they both offered me a realistic view of the challenges of growing as a couple, using their own relationship, their own struggles, their own ever-growing faith and belief when you allow yourself to be God's vessel. It was. . .no, it IS sooooo enlightening for them to offer their own courtship, honeymoon years, and "longsuffering" in order for me to receive a realistic image of what marriage is, what marriage needs to be, what marriage can be. I'm still thankful for their willingness to share the imperfections that contribute to perfecting a marriage. I praise God for my Uncle William and Aunt Hattie Hall!

Tracey Jackson

I can always feel the Love of God radiating from my Aunt Hattie and my Uncle Will. Even their voices are filled with love when they speak. May God bless your book and all who read it. Love you both.

Robert Watkins, TV 38 WHPR

I was no more than ten years old. We lived down the street from Mother Hall. She has been my spiritual mother since then. I did not understand but she explained and helped me receive the Holy Spirit. She talks to me, scolds me, but more than anything, prays for me. The only difference between her and my biological mother is my mother birthed me. Mother Hall helped raise me and taught me to have a spiritual life. She loves me as much now as she did then and gave me a life-lasting introduction to the Lord Jesus Christ. My heart broke and tears came to my eyes when people talked about Jesus. It did not make sense then or now, why a man who is so good got treated so bad. How could an innocent person, loved by so many get accused and nailed to a cross? Pilate had the power to set him free but washed his hands of all of it and said let them be. Mother Hall taught me to do right and when you do, there is a power that will do and be right by you, I don't care what you are going through. I have a very beautiful wife. She is a very, very good mother and a very good wife. Right now, it looks like I am going through a divorce and I am doing everything to prevent it, but it is out of my hands. I don't want that. But I pray for God to show me which way to go and only He is showing me what to do because there is no way for me to know what I know without Him showing me. I have accepted that. I can't explain it. I can't understand it. But I was taught to count it all joy and if it wasn't for the teachings of my parents, Mother Hall, my pastor, I could not deal with what I'm dealing with in my life. They all taught me this too shall pass. I just have to be willing to put what I'm going through at this time in Gods hand's and I am quite sure I know I will be all right!

I UNDERSTAND - Sister Rose Watkins

I received the gift of the Holy Spirit at 12 years old. At such a young age, knowing He answered made me rejoice. I went back a few times and told my mother and she said I could not go back. No matter how much I would say I want to go to Mother Hall's church, it did not register. But what did register with me was the reason I was chosen to go to her church. I had to be covered from there because of what I went through the rest of my life. When I had children, I brought them up under the teachings of the Church Of Our Lord Jesus Christ. I may have tripped and fallen but I ran back to Mother Hall and she would say, "Come daughter. We're going to tarry." I am going to take some more classes under Bishop Hall and I want to teach the young women what to do. Mother Hall would tell me what to do, I would be obedient. Bishop and Mother Hall turned out to be wonderful for me because of their wisdom and what they gave me.

Mother Constance (Connie) Wells

"Render therefore to all their dues; tribute to whom tribute is due; custom to who custom; fear to whom fear; honor to whom honor." (Romans 13:7)

"Those that be planted in the house of the Lord shall flourish in the courts of our God. They shall still bring forth fruit in old age: they shall be fat and flourishing; to show that the Lord is upright: He is my rock, and there is no unrighteousness in Him." (Psalm 93:13-15)

"To everything there is a season, a time to every purpose under the sun." (Ecclesiastes 3:1)

Bishop and Mother Hall - this is your season to reap from the hands of the Almighty God the harvest from the seeds of your ministry that you have sown. Your harvest from the fields are the souls that you have brought into the kingdom of God; and by those who are being blessed by that harvest and will continue to be blessed by the fruit from your labor. To minister in a distinctive biblical sense means "to serve" or "be a servant" - your model is and has been "Our Lord and Savior Jesus Christ" - who Himself said: For even the Son of man came not to be ministered unto, but to minister, and to give His life a ransom for many (Mark 10:45).

In my life your years of service have been demonstrated time and again. "Behold I will do a new thing; now it shall spring forth; shall ye not know it? I will even make a way in the wilderness, and rivers in the desert" (Isaiah 43:18-20).

Little did I realize on that Wednesday evening, February 23, 1972, that my season had arrived and God that had begun the work of a new creation in my life; which has remained for forty-five years. PRAISE GOD!!!

It was my second visit to "THE ARK" (former edifice of The Church of Our Lord Jesus Christ) located at 2341 E. Seven Mile Road at Goddard. I was there because the invitation had been extended by the pastor the previous Sunday to all those who were seeking salvation to return on the upcoming Wednesday night. Based upon what I had witnessed on that Sunday morning - I knew that I needed to be there because I wanted my wilderness journey to end. When the altar call was made by the pastor (the late Bishop William L. Bonner) emphasis was placed on those seeking the "Holy Ghost" to be first to come to the altar. I was among the first to arrive there. I was then directed by the pastor to go to this lady who was standing close by having the most beautiful inviting smile on her face. Her entire demeanor spoke of love and concern and in my mind, I wondered - why is she looking at me in this way and she doesn't even know me? Now, I know, but time and space will not permit me to share it, only that this lady with the beautiful smile and show of concern was Mother Hattie Hall who assisted in the birthing of this baby into the kingdom of God!

Through the ministry of Mother Hall, I was mentored and taught (by example) in the ways of holiness. She taught me that I was entering into a relationship with the Lord Jesus Christ and that this relationship would develop through the practice of the spiritual disciplines and biblical practicalities that would involve prayer, fasting, study of the Word, serving and operating in the gifts of the Holy Spirit for the perfecting of the Saints, the edifying of the body of Christ, and the work of the ministry. Bishop Hall is undoubtedly a premiere Bible scholar. Most of the biblical teaching and the understanding of biblical truths that have become my life have been because he has not handled the Word of God deceitfully but by the manifestation of the truth as the Holy Spirit has revealed the truths of scripture to him. There have been and are many instances in my life outside of me being a part of Solomon's Temple that she, in her wisdom, has been a voice of reason. I'll share a few. Her willingness to accompany me to Wichita, KS, when my father passed; accompanying me to the Secretary of State office to obtain my driver's license; taking me with her and Bishop Hall to my first ever state meeting. She has been my cheerleader and encourager more times than I can count. Finally, she and Bishop Hall have always been those two familiar faces in the crowd when you just need to know "THAT SOMEONE CARES!" You will always be in my HEART!

A REFLECTION OF THE HALLS AND ME! - Mother Barbara Pittman

I met Bishop and Mother Hall in 1974 when introduced to the Church of Our Lord Jesus Christ (COOLJC). I came to see the late Pastor Bonner and why other preachers not of his faith held him in such high esteem. I got my answer. After being filled with the Holy Ghost, I began to work with different auxiliaries in the church. In those days, you had to go to

164

"Newcomers Class" to learn the doctrine and what being filled with the Holy Ghost meant. It was where I came in contact with Elder Hall, who was a man who spoke very softly and with such warmth in his voice that he captured your attention right away. Later I met Mother Hall...the lady with the anointed hands! She would always rub my back while we she talked with a soft voice. I began to notice them together; he treated her with so much respect, they were friends as well as husband and wife. But it was not until doctors diagnosed my husband with cancer that I got to see just how dedicated they were to their calling.

In spite of the fact he wasn't saved, they would visit him, it seemed almost every day. The day before he passed, he was to get baptized by bishop in the tub in the hospital. They were there when doctors said he was close to leaving here...Bishop Hall would say "When I see you, I am looking at a miracle."

THEY SAID MY BABY WAS DEAD - Mother Alma Jean Lee

In 1976, I was 5 months pregnant and when I woke up during the night, I could not feel Sarah moving. When I got to the hospital, my stomach had gotten hard like a big basketball and they said there was no heartbeat and Sarah was dead but she had to come out on her own. Sunday morning, when Bishop and Mother Hall heard about it, they said they were coming to see me that day! I had faith and confidence they were bringing me communion even though they did not say that. I knew Sarah was going to be all right. Evening came and I wondered why they had not arrived, but I knew they were coming. I fixed my food tray up nice and put it in front of me.

I felt my baby move and my roommate told me we are going to believe the baby is alive! Bishop and Mother Hall came in and Bishop Hall gave me confirmation of what God said.

"It was your faith that brought us here. We have been so loaded down today we were just too tired. But we said we've got to make it there. We are going to give you Holy Communion."

"Oh Thank You Jesus! I know everything is all right."

When he gave me that flesh, I just knew Jesus was healing me. When he gave me the blood the baby flipped over and started kicking! That was 41 years ago and she is fine.

GOD SENT - Mother Jewel Gibson

Bishop and Mother Hall took time to go and visit my mother who was not saved. Mother Hall was a friend and true mother when I was at my lowest, always calling and encouraging me. She has taught me no matter what is going on, turn it over to Jesus. She taught me to pray and depend on no one but Jesus. Most of all I am grateful for true holiness and sharing her wisdom. The gold nuggets have pulled me through many situations.

55 YEARS AND STILL COUNTING - Mother Marie Greear

My boyfriend at the time, now my husband, was a part of Bishop Bonner's church at Orleans Street. My soul was not satisfied at my Presbyterian church and my husband said he wanted to take me to his church. He brought me to the COOLJC where I met Mother Hall with a spirit like nothing I've ever seen before. She taught all the women how to dress and be holy. From that day, she kept trying to make me the woman God wanted me to be. Sometimes I was angry with her, but did what she said and sometimes I was so happy I knew her because I married Willie Greear. She was the best person I could have had to teach me how to be a wife, giving instruction and living what she said. She told me to go visit the sick and call them on the phone if you can't go in person. Talk to them while doing housework and cooking, but don't neglect your husband. She nurtured me. Sometimes it was hard to love her and after all these years I don't regret that I kept loving and obeying her. With all of my family, Bishop and Mother Hall have been right there supporting us. My children thought we were blood related because they spent more time with the Hall's than with their own relatives. For decades, Mother Hattie Hall was the First Lady of Solomon's Temple because we did not have one. Although she was never accepted and respected as the First Lady, Mother Hall did everything the First Lady was supposed to do. She prayed us through dark times.

TRUE SERVANTS A LADY AND A GENTLEMAN - Mother Doris Little

I am so honored and proud to give tribute to Bishop William Hall and Mother Hattie Hall, a lady and a gentleman, true servants of the Lord, true servants of His people. I remember them both as far back as when I was 12 years old and as of this writing, I am 71 years old. Throughout all those years, God has been good to them, me and my family. I have seen them develop into people of good character integrity, dignity, working together diligently under the leadership of the late Chief Apostle, Bishop William Lee Bonner. Even through their trials and tribulations, they led souls to Christ. Their example of doing all they can for God's people has deeply inspired me and my family to be good courageous soldiers on the battlefield in God's Army. They continue doing so well all through prayer and with God's grace. Mother Hall and Bishop Hall show their love with actions, including bringing communion to my dear mother, Bernice Little, for many years. They prayed, sang songs, laughed and talked about old times together. I have no doubt those anointed blessed visits extended her life. Love does what nothing else can. Even when my mother moved in with me they came, climbing 15 steps! Thank God for Mother Hall and Bishop Hall. His lord said unto him, Well done, thou good and faithful servant: thou hast been faithful over a few things, I will make thee ruler over many things: enter thou into the joy of thy Lord (Matthew 25: 21).

VESSELS TO MINISTER - Sister Josette Harris

Mother Hall is a Godly woman who loves her husband and family and allows God to use her vessel to minister to many souls. I experienced the missions the Lord sent her on. If a saint was sick at home, we stopped at the fruit market and bought them fruit. We went to hospice and mental institutions. She is all about God's work. When Mother Hall sees a person in need, she tries to help that person. She pinned my clothing, disciplined, supported, taught me how to tarry with souls, how to set up the Communion Table. My experience with her is more than words can say and I love her.

MY MOTHER HALL - Mother Melson

This is the way I see my Mother Hall. She stands fast and unmovable in all her ways. Always doing work for the Lord which fits the life she lives, a close relationship with God. She is a soldier in her counsel for people. From Mother Hall, I have learned how to live for the Lord. I have worked with Mother Hall folding bulletins for 5 or 6 years and she has a Spirit of God like nobody else I have ever seen. I see her as being a sergeant for God. She is not a woman with many different faces and stands firm in her belief in God. Talking to her uplifts me. When she speaks, she has brought comfort to many, many people. She is in a class by herself.

SHE IS SO SWEET - Mother Joyce Redmond

Every Sunday Mother Hall hugged us and said come back. Her love drew us. I will never forget seeing her genuine concern and encouragement when she tarried with my sister. I was so comfortable with her because of how encouraging she was. Mother Hall had God given insight to encourage and used whoever God led her to use. At the end of Midnight Prayer, she always asked a minister to give a thought and asked Deacon Redmond for one before he became a minister because she saw his calling. I had a really ugly knot on my wrist that came up for no reason. There was no skin broken, but I was real self-conscious. I sat next to Mother Hall. She rubbed that knot and the next day it was gone and never came back.

We were ministers and deacons' wives before we were missionaries and Mother Hall taught us everything about missionary work. She was Vice President of the Missionaries and the Ministers and Deacons Wives. Bishop Bonner said we all had to go to the Missionary Department. Many needed additional teaching. When we walked in Mother Pandora Williams said, "I don't have to worry about this group. I know they were taught everything they need to know because Mother Hall taught them." She taught us to have the right mindset to prepare Holy Communion and how to be Ministers and Deacons Wives. She taught the proper way to visit the sick in teams of two with one praying aloud, the other one praying silently, because you can't be effective if both talk at the same time and don't stay too long. When working the altar make sure you have fresh breath and that your body is fresh. If not, you are offensive and a distraction. Mother Hall always has little things like safety pins, needle and thread, lotion, Kleenex, blessed oil, breath mints, and taught us to do the same. Ministers still ask the missionaries for blessed oil. Elder Redmond and I enjoyed Bishop Bonner's preaching but always looked forward to seeing Mother Hall. I never remember her saying I don't have time. You had to respect her time because Bishop Hall would be waiting at the door for her patiently while she was talking to people in church and he never complained. There were always people around Mother Hall. Mother Hall's love made the difference in many areas in my life.

STILL PARTNERS AFTER ALL THESE YEARS - Sister Glenda Reed

My life has been touched by Elect Lady Hattie Hall and Bishop William Hall to be under their leadership and work alongside them with Pastor Bonner. Thank you, Lord, for the miracle in the lives of your servants. I am so grateful you blessed them to grow into this season of their lives together. Many times one is left to finish the journey alone, but your grace has favored their lives, marriage, and work in your Kingdom. Thank you for the words of wisdom I receive from them and the example they have shown to so many of holiness and faithfulness.

I arrived in Detroit in 1979 after marrying Minister Arnold Reed on Christmas Day. Leaving all of my family behind and moving to a city where I knew no one caused me to feel alone. Mother Hall opened her arms, welcomed me to Solomon's Temple and made me feel like a daughter. I obtained a position in the church office which brought the opportunity to work daily with Mother and Bishop Hall. Every day of the week they left the church to go visit the sick and shut-in, often not returning until late afternoon; but when there was a need, they were there. I had to have surgery early in the morning and when I arrived at the hospital with Elder Reed, Bishop and Mother Hall were already there. To see the faithfulness of these two warriors did something to my heart. Working so closely with them gave me an upper hand. I saw their prayer life, love, obedience, and devotion to their pastor. Mother Hall is not ashamed to share her testimony knowing it has and will bless many others. Her testimony has changed young married women's lives and given hope to many mothers who have wanted to give up and throw in the towel. She speaks under the anointing even when sharing a testimony. Bishop Hall still finds himself working to help others in any way that he can. Every other Friday, he is out there distributing food to the community. "Sit down and rest a while...." is not in him. Bishop Hall loves God and God's people. His prayers definitely get through to God. Are the Hall's perfect? No, but they strive every day for perfection, and I know without a shadow of a doubt that when they stand before the Almighty God; He will say to them, "Well done my good and faithful servants." God Bless you Elect Lady Hattie Hall and Bishop William Hall.

SHE GETS A PRAYER THROUGH - Mother Willa Bowman

I met Mother Hall several years ago when I joined Solomon's Temple. She is the nicest and most considerate person I have ever met. I have called her many times to talk and she always listens to and prays for me. Recently, I called and told her during my annual physical when my doctor found a lump and I needed tests. She prayed for me and all of my tests came back good. The Lord has always heard and answered her prayers for my family. Mother Hall can get a prayer through for real! July, 2017, one of my family members was diagnosed with prostate cancer. Mother Hall prayed. The doctor told him to get radiation treatments and now he is healed of cancer.

A RARE GEM - Mother Willa Mae Snead

We met Mother Hattie Hall nearly 45 years ago. To say she is a rare gem is an understatement. She possesses those qualities in Proverbs 2 as well as the virtuous woman. She truly is a servant leader who teaches you to possess those qualities. A quiet and gentle spirit that presents strength in prayer and influence. It was good for me to have been with her. Out of her mouth is the law of kindness. She opens her mouth to wisdom and on her tongue is kindness (Proverbs 31:26).

GOD USES HER TO WORK MIRACLES - Mother Mary E. Talbert

I met Mother Hattie Hall 30 years ago. We used to go out on missions and before we could get back, she would remember others. She had the yearning to visit everyone she could. We went into a ward. Someone was near death. We began to pray and that person began to speak in tongues. Next, we saw a mother with weeks to live who wanted her daughter saved. Her daughter stayed and listened. We had prayer and Mother Hall told her come on; it's your time. Mother began to tell her to let it go and while her mother was going home to be with the Lord she began to speak in tongues. There is a special anointing God has given Mother Hall to work with souls and not let them go. She encouraged me to go out even when she could not go. She told me, "We all have to be able to speak to a soul to let them know that Jesus is the way, the truth and the life." Mother Hall thank you for our continual beautiful journey. She has been praying with my brother, Ben Avery in

McCormick, South Carolina for three months and after surgery and all is well. She prays everybody through.

GOD CHANGED MY NO TO YES - Mother Carolyn Taylor

Mother Hall is the first person that approached me when I walked into Solomon's Temple for the first time. I didn't know my husband warned her about talking to me about the baptism in Jesus' Name. Deacon Taylor's brother had received the Holy Ghost and his brother had a dream that he was speaking in tongues. He called us and said, What do I do in order to speak in these tongues that I dreamed about?" I was a happy Baptist girl and did not want to hear Mother Hall talk about being baptized in Jesus' name and receiving the gift of the Holy Ghost. I had recently been healed; my brother was Holy Ghost filled so I knew there was more than what I had. Mother Hall began to speak so beautiful and kind, my non-listening ears began to listen. She was ministering to my brother-in-law and his wife but every now and then she was leaning over looking at me. When she finished, my brother-in-law and Phyllis immediately said, "We're ready to go down in Jesus' name." I looked at all of them and I don't know what I was going to say, but before I knew it, I was saying, "Mother Hall, I believe in this baptism and I want to be baptized." I was expecting so as they took us to the baptism room and I said to myself, 'What's wrong with me? I've been baptized in the name of the Father, Son and Holy Ghost. Why am I trying to get baptized in Jesus' Name? But it was amazing when Bishop Hall baptized us in Jesus' name and for the very first time when I came up out of that water, I felt so clean and pure. Something happened that I couldn't explain, but I never felt that way before in my life, just being buried in Jesus' name. The rest is history. We tarried that night and I found out later I actually spoke in tongues. Because I didn't know I was speaking in tongues, nobody told me. But the next time on a Sunday morning in February, Bishop Bonner called for those who wanted the Holy Ghost. A sister came told me I tarried so beautifully the other night and she walked me back up to the altar which was full. Bishop Bonner walked down the steps and asked me.

"Daughter, what do you want?"
"I want the Holy Ghost! I want the Holy Ghost!"
And he said, "Believe!"

He began to rebuke satan and in 2 minutes, I was speaking in tongues. I was pregnant, stood there, didn't fall, roll or all those other things. I just stood and received the precious gift of the Holy Ghost. After 40+ years, I'm still saved, sanctified and Holy Ghost filled. I am so grateful for Mother Hall allowing the Lord to use her to speak to my heart. Bishop and Mother Hall changed my life by their obedience. Mother Hall told me the Holy Spirit told her, "You are talking to her brother-in-law but also speaking to her" and that has just really been a blessing in my life.

THE LOVE & TEACHING ARE ROOTED IN ME - Sister Helen Thurston

When I got saved in 1970, Elder Hall taught Newcomer's Class and wanted me to come but I was working and didn't have a car. When I got off work, Mother Hall had to go by her house, have dinner with them then she and Elder Hall would drive me to church and then home. She did this with me as a newcomer in the Lord so that I would be able to hear the Word of God. I enjoyed the class because I needed the teaching. Classes started at 6:30, lasted until 7:00 or 8:00 and it was 9:00 or 10:00 when they brought me home. They did this for years until I was able to get a car of my own. I learned a lot about the Bible which laid my foundation for my spiritual walk now. The love they showed me was so important because I needed someone to welcome me into the church. It was unforgettable and very special. This foundation gave me a hunger and thirst for the word, just like nourishment for your body. To this day, I am still hungry and thirsty to know the word because of the foundation Bishop and Mother Hall introduced to me when I first came to the church.

WHEN HE WAS 3 YEARS OLD, THEY MADE A DIFFERENCE - Brother Arthur Mason III

In 1959, my mother, Viola Mason, received the Holy Ghost at Church of Our Lord Jesus Christ under the pastorate of Bishop William Bonner. I was just three years old and Elder and Mother Hall played such a vital part in my growing up. My siblings and I attended school with their children. Kim and I even had the same piano teacher. Although Bishop Bonner was our pastor, I considered Bishop and Mother Hall my spiritual parents when church mothers had the authority to discipline, admonish and instruct any child in the church; Mother Hall did that and then some. I tarried with Bishop and Mother Hall, but it was Mother Hall's gentle encouragement and prayers that affected me greatly. In July 1984, I received God's most precious gift of all, the Holy Ghost in the presence of Mother Hall and I vividly remember her telling me, "You had it three days ago, we were just waiting for you to say it". I love Bishop and Mother Hall and pray that the Lord continues to shower them with blessings.

COME OUT FROM AMONG THEM - Dr. Charles Thompson

Friends went to the church and told me about the Power of God in the services. I wasn't going to leave Holy Cross because my grandmother was Apostolic. They joined church in the winter then left in the summer. I won't be a hypocrite. I told Bishop Bonner what was going on with me and my church and he told me to stay where I was until the Lord started dealing with me to come out from among them. They hadn't done anything to me, but my soul needed a change. Something happened at their convention and when I got back, the Lord said, 'You are out, stay out.' Mother Hall was my witness. On Monday, December 17, 1973, I went to church. Elder Ford from New York was the evangelist. After tarrying for the Holy Ghost, I came out and Sister Rose asked if I was Holy Ghost filled and I said, "I don't know". They had the seekers to tell what they got. I went to the altar and requested that the saints pray that I get the Holy Ghost. Elder Hall looked so disappointed. I came home and talked to the Lord. "Lord, I asked for the Holy Ghost, but I guess it's not for me." I started fixing breakfast-sausage and cereal. When I started the sausage, I took my hand off the skillet and felt the Lord. Thank you, Jesus! I went in my room and that is when the

Holy Spirit came on me stronger and I started waving my hands and speaking in tongues. I had to tell somebody! Mother Hall answered the phone and started praying. "Lord whoever it is, release them so they can tell me who they are." "This is Charles! I got the Holy Ghost!" "Do you want me to wake Elder Hall up and let him see if you got the Holy Ghost?" "No, I know I've got it!" They came to my house a few years later after I went to the foot doctor and they wanted to do another surgery. When I went back to have the second surgery, they found no cancer at all.

PEACE IN THE MIDST OF THE STORM - Brother Romell Travics

No moment is more raw, painful, harrowing, sensitive and fragile than when a family who must face making funeral arrangements for a loved one. At best, there are raw emotions, confusion and not a lot of understanding. At worst, there are a lot of tears, arguing, lashing out at anyone who is there - including representatives of the Death and Comfort Ministry of the Church. Mother Hattie Hall was ALWAYS the voice of reason, peace, calm in these situations. No matter what else goes on in those meetings, Mother Hall was able to do the impossible. Her prayer and patience always calms the families. At that point, they would listen. This clears the way for me to handle the necessary business. This includes providing detailed information about every phase of this delicate process. We provide available options for honorable, dignified, and reverent burial of their loved one. When we are finished, families are always left with the encouragement and knowledge that they are not alone. They know they have a partner in Solomon's Temple that will be with them every step of the way. Mother Hattie Hall truly brings peace in the midst of every storm!

MEMORIES - Mazzie Denise Graham-Booker

I have known the Hall family over 55 years and my family loves them as blood relatives because of the love and kindness they have shown us over the years. I remember Bishop Hall was one of the first black managers of A&P in Hamtramck. My siblings and I were sitting on our front porch steps waiting and watching for this wonderful, handsome man to come and bring the "blessing" of his presence and jelly donuts. Knowing him now, those kind words, prayers and treats were him sowing seeds for "souls." When Bishop Hall left A&P and was called by the Lord to serve Bishop Bonner until his death, I knew the treats would cease, but that is how a child thinks.

Mother Hall has always been a soft-spoken "powerhouse" with the Lord working through her. She works quietly bringing souls to Christ, encouraging and instructing young women on holy living. She always made herself available even while taking care of her family and going through persecution. I cannot count the many times I witnessed Mother and Bishop in Hospitals praying for souls to receive "salvation." They served and prayed for the sick and shut-in, served communion in hospitals and homes, visited the bereaved and ministered to souls with no regrets and no complaints. Mother and Bishop Hall have been good stewards over souls and understand their reward for all of their faithfulness, love, loyalty will not be received in this life, but in Glory where they will receive extra stars in their crowns for all the work they have done in the Lord's garden.

UP CLOSE AND PERSONAL - Sister Deborah Reese

When I came to Solomon's Temple so many years ago, I had the rare privilege to become Bishop Bonner's secretary, which meant secretary of the church and all of the ministers. From that day, I have had a front row seat to the ministry, lives, changes and gifts of Mother Hattie Hall and Bishop William Hall. Because I am in the office, I receive many of the requests for prayer, counseling and help. It never ceases to amaze me how willing, patient and kind Mother Hall and Bishop Hall are to EVERYONE! They leave church in the morning and sometimes don't get back until later in the evening and they are yet concerned about the people of God - and never complain!

Bishop Hall fields countless requests for prayer and an innumerable amount of questions about life, the Bible, ministerial conduct and more from members, ministers, everyone! He has the patience and understanding to give of himself continually. Perhaps one of my greatest blessings has been working in the office with Mother Hall. Her anointing, wisdom and presence bring a calmness to a very active environment. No matter the events or people, Mother Hall never fails to show love, patience and when called upon, pray for those who are in need. She never allows anything or anyone to upset her. It is a privilege to be with her. The greatest blessing of all, is watching the team all these years.

There are not many things that are consistent in life. The church has grown and Bishop and Mother remain faithful, consistent and caring about all of us. I know. I have a front row seat. May God bless and keep you both!

THE EPITOME OF HOLINESS - Brother Gregory Brown

What can I say about Mother Hattie Hall? Well she is the epitome of holiness. I thank the Lord for Mother Hall whom I affectionately call "Mama". She was one of the first missionaries I encountered when I first started visiting COOLJC (Seven Mile) in 1968. She has been an intricate part of my spiritual growth ever since. I developed a relationship with God by attending her Midnight Prayer every Friday night after youth services. I thank God because He has ordained Mother Hall to be a mentor to me all these years. I love you Mother Hall and pray that God will continue to bless you and your ministry!!!!

THEY ARE AN INCREDIBLE TEAM - Sister Laura M. Watson

Mother Hall is a "very" skilled, and wonderfully competent missionary! Bishop Hall is a passionate and astute "lover" of the WORD of God! Remembering their kindness to me in the past.

MOTHER HATTIE HALL, WHO IS SHE?
Pastor Lovell & Lady Tina Cannon

In our lives, she is a woman who hears God and takes Him at His word! An example of a lady, wife, mother, confidante. A woman who knows her God will answer! She has taught us the blessing in laboring at the altar with souls to be filled with the gift of the Holy Ghost. She doesn't hesitate to inform you that "she will put the power of prayer on you." Her teachings and continuous words of inspiration have blessed our lives. "Receive my instruction, and not silver; And knowledge rather than choice gold. For wisdom is better than rubies" (Proverbs 8:10-12).

Watching and learning from the tireless days of her and Bishop Hall visiting the sick at homes or at the hospital bedside taught my husband and I how to have compassion and strength to pray for those in need. Oh, what a beautiful woman she is! What an impact she has made in the Kingdom of God! We love and appreciate you very much! Blessings!

MY GODMOTHER - Anthony Derbah II

Mother Hall is my wonderful Godmother and a staple at Solomon's Temple. Throughout my youth to adulthood on Communion Sundays I always searched for my Godmother with the warm smile and gracious heart sitting in the second row close to the pulpit. Even though I currently reside in the DC Metro area, whenever I'm in Detroit and attending Solomon's Temple service, I seek the word and my Godmother.

OVER 50 YEARS OF WORKING TOGETHER - Sister
Freddie Derbah

While tarrying, Mother Hall finished tarrying with someone
else, got up to talk to our small group and danced in the spirit.
I never saw anybody dance like that before or after. I wanted
that and soon received the Holy Ghost. I was smoking and
wanted to quit and when I got the Holy Ghost that day the
Lord took my desire for cigarettes with no side effects. I still
remember her teachings from the Newcomer's Class. She and
Bishop Hall have an amazing prayer life. I did not have a car
and they always took me to the bus stop or downtown all the
way home and even to their house where Mother Hall cooked
me breakfast. Bishop Hall taught so well that even as a new
Christian, I understood everything he said. His words were
always from the Bible and food to my soul. After I had my
first child, Mother Hall took care of him for months until my
mom came to babysit for me and never charged me. They
watched out for everyone. I was out of service a while because
of work and life situations. I went back to church and Bishop
Hall said he was worried about me. That made me look at
myself because he would not have said it unless there was a
reason. I thank God for being able to sit down with them.
They always treat me like one of their daughters. Their prayer
life taught me to that when you learn how to talk to the Lord
you get things done, you know where you are and that has
brought me through every day of my life.

MONTHLY FOOT WASHING - Rochelle Dudley

Bishop and Mother Hall have been faithful clients for 20 years at my salon where I give them pedicures, unbeknownst to them, it is monthly foot washing blessed of the Lord. I truly believe their presence, prayers, blessings and words of encouragement play a major part in my 20 years of success.

Lucretia Batten-Knight

"For whosoever shall call upon the name of the Lord shall be saved" (Romans 10:13 KJV).

It was 40 years ago that I accepted Jesus Christ as my personal Lord and Savior! The word of God says: "In whom ye heard the word of truth, the gospel of your salvation: in whom also after that ye believed, ye were sealed with that Holy Spirit of promise" (Ephesians 1:13 KJV). August 8, 1978 was truly that day for me. Back in the day, it was required of us to "tarry" (which means to wait) or to consistently call on the name of Jesus in order to receive the Holy Spirit. So I did.

We used to have to travel about an hour from where we lived, to the Church Of Our Lord Jesus Christ, better known as Solomon's Temple. My parents would bring my sister and me to our Godmother's house, where our brother, Greg, would come and pick us up and take us to the Thursday night live broadcast. I remember those services were so powerful! This particular night, our pastor, the late Bishop William L. Bonner, was preaching and his subject was something like, "A Ship is about to Sink." I remembered it was about a ship because I knew that I didn't want to be on that ship! I was so emotional and excited about receiving the Holy Ghost.

After his message, Bishop Bonner made the altar call. If I recall correctly, those who wanted to receive the Holy Ghost were taken to the upper room. Mother Hattie Hall and Sherri White-Young, along with others, accompanied us to the upper room. In those days, Mother Hattie Hall and the late Mother Pandora Williams were considered (to me) to be two of the Fab Five Prayer Warriors in the war room. If one of them were praying with you, it was a guarantee that the windows of heaven were going to be opened wide! They were on their knees, praying for me as I called out the name of Jesus, I remember quite a few things came across my mind…"It's getting late!" We're going to have to get back to my Godmother's house because my parents are going to leave us and who's up here in the upper room with me? I became even more emotional because I really wanted God to fill me with His Holy Spirit. I believed that I was going to receive it that night. I did not want to leave the church without it!

After a period of time had passed, it was getting late and they were getting ready to close the upper room. Mother Hall, and others, helped me to my feet as I continued to cry and call on the name of Jesus. They walked me out into the hall, and as we stepped on the elevator, Mother Hall said to me, "The Lord can give you the Holy Ghost, even on the elevator!" Just moments stepping on the elevator, I begin to speak in unknown tongues and was filled with His Holy Spirit at that moment! I ran into the bulletin room as we got off the elevator and round the sanctuary, full of joy unspeakable, praising

God for this wonderful, precious gift that I had longed to have for 10 years! That Sunday when I took the right hand of fellowship, Bishop Bonner named me "the elevator baby." Thank you, Mother Hall (Bishop Hall) for your many years of service, for being a true servant of God and allowing Him to use you mighty fully!

THOUSANDS FILLED! - Brother Hershel Dunn, Jr.

I appreciate the fellowship and prayer of Mother Hattie Hall and Bishop William Hall for over 40 years. Saints have witnessed thousands of souls filled with the precious gift of the Holy Ghost. My family petitioned our prayer band to agree for Jesus' healing of my cousin when a car battery exploded in his face, blinding him and Jesus Christ healed him from that terrible accident.

I KNOW WHERE I WAS ON 9/11 - Brother Glenn Ford

On 9/11, I had an appointment with Bishop and Mother Hall for prayer because I was having eye surgery the following week and I felt very relieved after they prayed that I would not need the surgery. I had a detached retina and holes because of being beaten during a carjacking and there was a very high probability that I would go blind. I had the surgery and it was a complete success! I follow up every year, I have 20/20 vision and need nothing else.

FAITHFUL SERVANTS TO THREE GENERATIONS - Sister Jimmie Foster

When my husband was in a nursing home, Bishop and Mother Hall visited, prayed for him and brought Bishop Bonner to pray. Without them, there would have been no minister to pray for him. When my husband died, Bishop Hall eulogized him and Mother Hall was nurse, missionary and usher at the funeral! When I asked her to pray for my son, she and Bishop Hall prayed and we got the victory. We could not have made it without them.

THEY SET CHRISTIAN LIVING EXAMPLES - Deacon David Lewis

Thank God for this opportunity to say words of encouragement on behalf of Bishop and Mother Hall about the past 42 years that I have been a member of Solomon's Temple. Bishop and Mother Hall set many examples for Christian living for saved people at Solomon's Temple Church. I have taken Bishop Hall's classes of Bible Fundamentals 1 and 2 which increased my understanding of God's word while giving me more boldness to speak. Mother Hall is a wonderful teacher of God's word and one of the Weeping Women. I went to her Midnight Prayer at Solomon's Temple and watched her tarry with many seeking the Holy Ghost including family and friends. They are an anointed team working for the same goal. How can two walk together except they agree (Amos 3:3).

Sister Renita Foster

In my youth I was very active at Solomon's Temple and very close to Bishop and Mother Hall. For several years I have not attended services, but Bishop and Mother Hall never forgot me and never stopped loving me. Recently I had a major problem and NOBODY could help me. My mother asked Bishop and Mother Hall to pray for me. They called me, prayed, treated me as if I never left, never asked for details and did not repeat it to anyone. They yet hold me in their hearts with their prayers. It does not matter how far away I am, or how long it is, to know someone loves me that much and I am still their daughter in the Lord speaks volumes of their genuine Christlike love. Never will I forget. God worked it out and all is well!

SHE DISCIPLINED WITH LOVE – Karen Grace White-Furcron

She disciplined with love. I remember her trying to make me wear whole slips and she didn't quite know how to deal with me. She said, "Baby, now you need to cover up. I can see through the back of your blouse." You know my mouth was terrible. I don't remember verbatim but it wasn't nice. She never held my mouth against me. I really thank God for the Mother Hall's of the world. She allowed me space to mature and that I did. I love Mother Hattie Hall.

THE MORNING GLORY - Sister Sherri F. White-Young

My salvation experience on July 29, 1965 was a Tuesday morning that started like most Tuesday mornings in my grandmother's house. We were staying there while my mother went to work. Most mornings at her house we would have "Granny's hearty breakfast" but not Tuesday mornings. She was the chaplain for the Missionary Department and the missionaries had noon day prayer on Tuesday's in the prayer room at the Church of Our Lord Jesus Christ on the corner of Halleck and Dequindre. She fasted and we "fasted" right along with her. My sister Grace and I went with her to service. She was serious about her responsibility. Regardless of who showed up, my granny would have church. We would pray, sing, read the word and go home. This Tuesday, Mother Pandora Williams and Mother Hattie Hall were both there. The five of us had service! That day was life-changing for me. I was 11 years old. I even remember what I was wearing - a navy blue sailor dress with a white collar and a red ribbon belt. When prayer began, as it was the custom, we began to tarry. There were several other young people who had recently received the Holy Ghost. I was jealous. They were new to the church. I had been there since I was 3 months old. How could they get it before I did? Soon those thoughts were gone. I was earnestly seeking God. I could hear Mother Hall encouraging me - "Come on baby, praise Him. Let Him have His way!" What a wonderful experience. They were such encouragers. I received the Holy Ghost that very day. My sister Grace, not to be outdone, received it the next day. We had the privilege of praying with and learning from such a great powerhouse. We watched Mother Hall care for her husband, her children, and her church. What a testament to both greatness and humility.

TRY ONE MORE TIME - Elder Gary R. Gay, Sr.

I was sick and tired of drinking, smoking, partying and my soul was thirsty. God was dealing with me but I didn't understand what it was about. I came to Noah's Ark for the Thursday night broadcast, got baptized and tarried for about a week in 1974. I had given up everything because I wanted this Holy Ghost needed a change in my life. I got to church, tarried and didn't receive it. My friends invited me to a cabaret that night. Since I could not get the Holy Ghost, I told Mother Hall the Holy Ghost is not for me. I'm going to the cabaret with my friends. She told me to try one more time. In six seconds, I was filled with the Holy Ghost!

They called me a preacher but I wasn't looking to be a preacher. I never missed Mother Hall's Midnight Prayer. One night a young lady who came in that needed deliverance and when we began to pray with her she started crawling under the pews, hissing and slithering like a snake. We prayed and pleaded the blood and that snake spirit left out of her. Her countenance was radiant when God set her free. All of my friends and family came to salvation through Midnight Prayer. It was the place to be on Friday Night from Midnight until 3:00 a.m. Bishop Hall was right there tarrying with the brothers, laying on hands or laying prostate, crying out to God for souls. He never left her side. Midnight Prayer is the foundation of my prayer and I still believe in laying before

God in prayer for everything. Bishop Bonner taught me if you pray, God will give you everything you want and supply your needs according to His riches in glory. Circumstances and suffering don't pull you away but draw you to God through prayer. Bishop and Mother Hall learned through Bishop Bonner how to pray the same way I did. Midnight Prayer enhanced what was already there. Bishop Bonner's example of prayer and Mother Hall working with the souls together have been a great conduit in my deliverance ministry.

I DON'T KNOW IF YOU REMEMBER - Sharon Seaborn

To my precious spiritual mother, Hattie Hall, I'm not sure if you remember it; however, you have been an integral part of my life from the very beginning, starting with my spiritual birth when I received the gift of the Holy Ghost in 1982. I was so drunk in the Spirit that you took me in your arms, like mothers do when their child is in need and laid my head on your lap. That was an awesome day. It was at that moment that our lives were interwoven and you truly became my spiritual mother. Your guidance, throughout the years that followed, has been immeasurable. When I became a Junior Missionary, you were there to teach me the ropes, after which I went on to become a Senior Missionary. Also, Mother, when you gave me the opportunity to assist you in writing some of your messages, this led me to really study the word and it was instrumental in creating that hunger in me for the word of God. You saw in me what I didn't even see in myself at that time. Secondly, on the many occasions that I had the opportunity, to ride with you and Bishop Hall, I watched and listened to your interactions with your husband. You were teaching me then, and you didn't even know it. You had so much wisdom, and I was eager to glean some. I thank you for the opportunity just to sit with you in those early years to learn how to be a Godly praying wife. I felt as though we were Naomi and Ruth. Thirdly, it would be remiss of me if I didn't mention your powerful prayer life. I learned that from you as well, (all those nights in Midnight Prayer). Little did I know that I would need that prayer life to conquer the many trials that would ensue throughout the course of my spiritual journey and for that, I am eternally grateful to you. In my eyes, you have truly been that Proverbs 31 woman, and I know that my life has been blessed immensely because of it, and yes, I do rise up and call you "blessed". I will always remember the lessons that you taught me, those spoken and unspoken. Lastly, thank you Mother Hall, for allowing me to be one of your daughters. Not many women can say that they had a great mentor, but I can truly say that you were the best and my life is eternally enriched. I love you and may the Lord continue to bless you and give you strength because strength and honor are truly your clothing.

MY GOD CHOSEN GOD-MOTHER, MOTHER HATTIE HALL Your Godson, Servant Phil Hamiel

". . .an apple tree among wood trees" (Song of Solomon 2:3)

When I was first asked to write something in Mother Hall's book, I was instantly overwhelmed with the feelings of inadequacy to be chosen to say something about this mother in Zion who is a spiritual giant in her own right. This is the mother who demons recognize and do not want you to tell her anything that would push her to her knees. For it is there that many of the battles that they have waged have been met with the most humiliating yet victorious defeats from the prayers of this great mother in Zion. Yet, at the same time I knew within myself that our close relationship was one that was established by God himself. It is one that she nor I chose, but He chose for His glory for which I am so forever grateful to God.

Knowing assuredly that God was the author of our kindred mother and son bond, we never looked-for consent from man for what God had established (me being her Godson). Neither did we find it necessary to publicize it, for it was something we both knew and we did not need to make sure man was on board with it. See when God does something you don't need man's approval or validation, you just need to be sure beyond a doubt that it's God. If you find that you do need man's approval, I would go pray again to be sure you're hearing from God. If the findings are that you are indeed hearing from God then impressing man is irrelevant – Selah.

Mother Hall's story with me began at my former church before I even knew who she was. God was even then setting something in motion in my life with her in mind. You see the Lord had begun directing me to leave my former church and did not let up until I did. But here is the thing, He did not tell me where to go. Ah Lord God! I can understand how Abraham felt when you said to him, "Go to a land that I WILL SHOW YOU". I finally obeyed God not knowing what church I was to attend. I was scared beyond reason for I was not under a covering, in which I am a strict believer. But I would soon find out that God's covering is universal and not building limited and He will care for you in these types of situations. Again, I say in these types of situations until He plants you in the church where He wants you to be. But again only when He's leading you to leave - Selah.

I worked midnights during this time and had been led by God to attend Midnight Prayer conducted by Mother Hall. I did not belong to the church (The Ark Church), not even the organization, but God told me to go pray there and I did without question. I attended Midnight Prayer for about six months not knowing that God was setting me up to plant me at the place of my ultimate destiny. I was working afternoons at this time and would make a beeline to Midnight Prayer right after work but would always leave about 15 minutes before prayer ended because I did not want to speak to anyone. (I thought the saints there were very spiritual but a little on the wired side). One night after work, I went to Midnight Prayer. This particular night was different somehow because the heaviness in my spirt from the weight of God not telling me where to go had become unbearable. If you think waiting on God is easy, it is not and can push you to your wits end. I want to pause here and say that I had attended a few churches, but God would not speak with the clarity I was used to, so I could and would not join – Selah. Oh, but this night God had a surprise for me, which was my answer. When I reached Midnight Prayer I was praying silently, sobbing to God for direction but again He said nothing. And as usual right before prayer ended, I got up and jetted out, tears streaming down my face like water. When I got to my car and put my hand on the door to open it, I heard this sweet voice say "Young man, young man". I turned around and there was Mother Hall standing in the doorway of the church. I said "Yes?" She said "Can I speak to you for a minute?" I really didn't want to, but took my hand off the car door and went to her. She said ever so sweetly, but with so much Godly assurance, "The Lord told me to tell you this is the place." "The place?" "Yes." "In prayer, He told me you have been waiting on Him to tell you what church to make your home and told me to tell you this is the place."

Now, don't forget I did not know her nor anyone at the church and I had not discussed my situation with anyone so she could not have known. I was birthed into what is now called Solomon's' Temple over 35 years ago through Mother Hattie Hall. The mother who God used to put me under my destined Pastor, Bishop William L. Bonner, whose spiritual DNA lives in me richly. He was the pastor of my destiny and mother was the midwife used to bring me under him. I was already saved and filled with the Holy Ghost. I got the Holy Ghost like they did in the Bible days. It fell on me coming up out of the water baptism in Jesus' name. I never tarried for it. I did not even know what tarrying was because I had never seen it. God just gave it to me right in the water! Being Birthed into the kingdom in one thing and only God can do that. But being birthed and adjoined to your God chosen pastor is another. Mother Hall was used to bring me into my God chosen destiny and that is why she is truly my GOD-mother, not the conventional Godmother name we are used to. There is nothing wrong with that, because I am even a Godfather as we speak and not in name only but actions. However, she is a mother God used to birth me into my destiny.

Mother Hall, you are an apple tree among wood trees. In other words, I have known many Zion mothers in my 38 years of being saved (35 of them knowing you) but none compare to you. You stand out, you shine, you pray, you love, you help, you bless, you support, you smile, you encourage, you console, you correct and you do it all ever so sweetly. I love you God-Mom and thank you for obeying God's voice to speak something to a young man trying to find God's will for his life and through you I found it. In the words of my late father in the gospel, "I love you bushels and barrels and cup running over!" I appreciate you so much my dear Godmother, the mother chosen by God to move me from one level of faith to the next.

OH WHAT THEY HAVE MEANT TO ME!
Brother Ellis Taylor

After I received the Holy Ghost, they took me home that night so I didn't have to catch the bus. Bishop Hall in Newcomer's Class explained 10% tithes instead of dues, fasting without telling anyone and more. I worked with guys who challenged everything I was doing.

"Why do you have to get baptized again?"
"I was baptized in the name of the Father Son and Holy Ghost and I had to be baptized in the Name of the Lord Jesus Christ."

Elder Hall studied and explained real good and did whatever Bishop Bonner said without arguing and never regretted leaving A&P. They were always together shopping and when they went to the hospitals. He would tell us, your wife is your help meet and has feelings, treat her right. I never knew him to be angry even when people tried to argue with him. They raised their children to treat other young people nice. They are real kind people to everybody and a mother and father to me. I always looked for him and Mother Hall when I came to church and they looked for me. When I would stay away from church, Bishop Hall would come by and tell me, "Brother Taylor, if you fall don't just lay there. Get up." My wife wanted to tarry real bad one night. She called and asked Mother Hall to meet her at church. We had six inches of snow and she did not have a lot of money. She told the cab driver she was going to church to tarry for the Holy Ghost and did not have enough money for the entire trip. She asked him to take her as far as he could with the money she had and she would walk the rest of the way. God touched his heart so he took her all the way. She got to church and in just a little while the Holy Ghost came in.

Mother Lottie Stewart

I have been a shut in for over a year, but before that I was in and out of the hospital like it was a revolving door. When Mother Hall got to the place where she could not walk down the hall, Bishop Hall put her in a wheelchair for her to see me. I turned 97 years old in February 2018.

Mother Hall does not let more than a week or two go by without calling, praying, singing a song, asking me to sing and we have a good time praising God on the phone. I love and appreciate her faithfulness. I can't come to church and it means something when people think about you. We forget but she doesn't forget.

THEY DID NOT LET HIM GO! - Sister LaWanda Rogan

My husband was having problems Sunday morning. I called 911 and tried to call church but no answer. My daughter went to church and told Elder Hall and he asked what was wrong with him and she said I don't know. When they got to our house, Elder Hall got out of the passenger side and asked what was wrong. I told him my husband is not breathing and they've got him in the ambulance. He began to pray with me waited with us at the hospital until we got a diagnosis. The doctor said he was having a series of massive heart attacks and they might have to take him to surgery to find out what's wrong. Bishop Hall sat in the room with our family while waiting to hear an answer. Around 11:00 a.m., we were still sitting in the waiting room waiting for an answer and Mother Hall walks in pushing Mother Pandora in a wheelchair and said, "Baby we came to sit with you. Everything is going to be alright."

After my husband died twice the doctor said by some miracle he is back. Bishop Hall left Sunday School to come be with us and did not leave our side until they knew Eddie was doing okay. They went in and prayed for him. Some other family members came and asked if he could pray and he prayed again. It was not until they went in and saw him for themselves, and that he was okay, that they left. I couldn't believe it!

SERVE RATHER THAN BE SERVED
Bishop Richard Snead

Bishop William Hall comes to serve rather than to be served. He exemplifies the true essence of a servant. Bishop Hall embraces the writings of Jesus when He said I came to serve rather than be served. Being a pastor myself, it is a rare quality to find someone who is as devoted to you, the man and the mission of the church. He is a faithful leader committed and dedicated to the success and mission of God's church. He carries on these attributes with a spirit of love.

A good man deals graciously and lends; He will guide his affairs with discretion. Surely he will never be shaken; The righteous will be in everlasting remembrance. He will not be afraid of evil tidings; His heart is steadfast, trusting in the Lord (Psalm 112:5-7).

Two are better than one; because they have a good reward for their labour (Ecclesiastes 4:9).

A MOTHER OF MANY - Sister Wendy Mitchell

Good works, light, example, faithful, steadfast, art, jewel, rock, sunshine, field of flowers, newborn baby, mountain, water, star at night, new pair of shoes, fresh hairdo, rain after a drought, the color of leaves in the fall, snow falling on your face in winter, laughter of children, family reunion, the spirit of love, joy and peace. You are all that and a bag of chips. Love, your daughter in the Lord.

THEIR CHILDREN BEAR WITNESS - Karen Shelton

About 15-20 years ago, I was working with a young lady that became my friend and daughter with an awesome personality. I called her Lisa. We shared the Word of God and many things about how good He is. My mother became ill and was hospitalized. When I told my friend, Lisa, she told me that her parents, Bishop and Mother Hall, had a ministry for visiting the sick. Wow!

My denomination was Baptist. I was so amazed they placed my mother's name on their prayer list and went to visit her at the hospital. I know we are all part of the body of Christ, but denominations separate us. To see this in action was the most eye-opening evidence of God's love through the Halls. It did not matter if my mother or I were a part of their church. Years after I left that place of employment, co-workers in my new employment would talk about God and ask where they fellowshipped. When they said Solomon's Temple, I asked about the Halls. Their response was MOTHER HALL and told how she prayed with them giving love and direction.

PROOF! - Larry Shirley

Mother Hall is proof that God has angels on earth.

I WILL ALWAYS LOVE HER - Carole Stallings

Mother Hall will always be very near and dear to my heart. She tarried with me when I received the Holy Ghost and helped me with each of my four children. I could sense someone was praying for me and Mother Hall would always say, "I've been praying for you". I had four children, was working at Comerica Bank and going to college. She would always encourage me by telling me "It's going to get better". She always had an encouraging word and scripture. She reminded me a lot of my mother. My mother is still living and no matter how bad it got, she would always say "It's going to get better". From 1980 until now, she still calls just to check on me and give me encouragement.

WONDERFUL! - Makeba Cawthon

Bishop Hall and beautiful Mother Hall have shown commitment to exemplify this passage in their daily lives! "Let this mind be in you, which was also in Christ Jesus" (Philippians 2:5).

SHE TAUGHT ME EVERYTHING! - Elder Charles Simmons

She is a good teacher who always had time for me. I knew nothing before I met Mother Hall. She always said, "Oh, there is my boy." I learned a lot from her. Bishop Hall helped me to understand people and be a better minister of God's Word.

SHE IS MY GODMOTHER - JoAnn Williams

I met Mother Hall in 1979 when I received the Holy Ghost. She taught me to be a holy woman and was an encouragement for my family, especially when my son was hit by a car. My mother passed when I was six years old and I thank Mother Hall for filling in that gap. Thank God for her enthusiasm, tenacity going through difficulties and continuing to rise with nothing but the grace of God. I thank her for being the prayer warrior and teaching the young women how to be women of God.

Behind every great woman is a great man and I thank God for Bishop Hall supporting Mother Hall in everything she endeavors to do. When my son was hit by a car, I had to pray and she taught me how to be persistent with God and get a prayer through. When we go before God, we have to know God is going to hear and answer our prayers. We must learn to wait because it is in God's time not ours. I thank her for teaching me how to be patient. She taught me how to dress, stay humble, be a first-class Woman of God. Continue doing the good works of the Lord.

Loisten Moore

MAMMA & DADDY HALL are the sweetest people I have known in Solomon's Temple. They have been a blessing in my entire life. The two of them are teachers walking in CHRIST. If you want to know anything you can always talk to Bishop & Mother Hall. I love them and thank GOD for them.

Rita Maggott

Mother Hall is a jewel. She is a very sweet person who loves GOD and I love her for that because she taught me how to love GOD. Mother Hall is a PRAYER WARRIOR. I was one of her Prayer Warriors from leading testimony service and tarrying with souls. She taught me how to tarry with souls in Midnight Prayer 'til they fully come through. She taught me the right way - not to tell them, but allow them to tell us that they were saved with the Holy Ghost. She is a jewel. I'm so grateful for her being in my life. I love her. So precious to me. She taught me a lot.

THE MOTHER OF BEAUTY - Sister Janette Mccuien

Someone said a Black woman is the 'The Mother of Beauty'. The Holy Spirit guided me many years ago to Solomon's Temple Church from the Kingdom Hall of Jehovah's Witnesses. I felt lost, in search of truth, full of pain, very bold and distrustful of church people. For many years no matter how overly bold I was in my beliefs, Mother Hall would put her most anointed hands on me and pray for me. So many times, I wanted to leave Solomon's Temple. One day Mother Hattie Hall told me, if you leave Solomon's Temple, you will lose your blessing. She said a few years later I reminded her of Ruth. Her words full of the Holy Spirit went into my heart and I submitted to the Holy Ghost. *Intreat me not to leave thee. . .whither thou goest, I will go; where thou lodgest, I will lodge: thy people shall be my people, thy God my God: Where thou diest, will I die, and there will I be buried (RUTH 1:16-17).*

SHE IS ALWAYS THERE - Jacqueline McDonald

She was there when I was down and out. When my daughter died last year, I wanted to call people, but my phone rang and it was Mother Hall. Hallelujah! She always attends funerals and ministers to the family. I was frustrated when I lost my brother, and she made everything alright. That was important to me because when my brother died, I couldn't even get out of the bed. Bishop Hall was there also. They always look out for you and Mother Hall tries to do what the Bible says. Nobody knows but God shows her when I am down and out and she loves, prays, and comes to me bringing love, help, hope, prayer and food. She tried to help in every way she could. She is just a splendid saint.

Bishop and Mother Hall with their daughters

Delphine and her family

Janese

Kim and her family

Lisa and her family

KOREA

William Hall in Korea

Army buddies

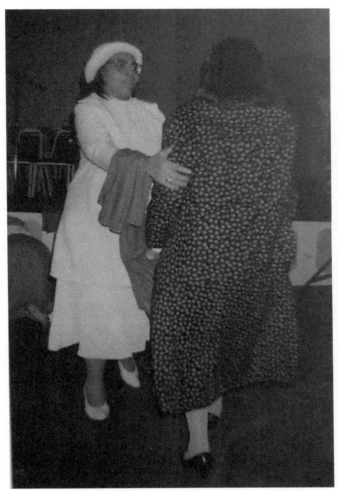

Mother Hall working with a soul

About The Authors

Highly esteemed and loved by all, Bishop William G. Hall and Mother Hattie Hall are the epitome of good and faithful servants. From serving as assistant pastor under the late Chief Apostle Bishop William L. Bonner at Solomon's Temple in Detroit, Michigan to now serving under the leadership of Bishop Doctor Henry, IV and Doctor First Lady Pamela Davenport to leaving a spiritual inheritance with their own family, this couple has served the Lord in excellence for over 50 years. Their legacy includes four daughters, eight grandchildren, nine great grandchildren, along with an abundance of spiritual children they've nurtured.

CPSIA information can be obtained
at www.ICGtesting.com
Printed in the USA
BVHW040525230222
629775BV00011B/893

9 781954 274075